Lonely Planet

POCKET

GENOA &
CINQUE TERRE

TOP SIGHTS · LOCAL EXPERIENCES

D1383120

REGIS ST LOUIS

Contents

Plan Your Trip 4

Welcome to Genoa & Cinque Terre

Italy's breathtaking Riviera is both a deeply historic destination and a fabulously in-the-moment pleasure-seeking one, where you can explore lavish *palazzi* (mansions) or humble village churches and then simply swim, eat, walk or gaze at the sea. Expect dramatic coastal topography, beautifully preserved architecture and one of Italy's most memorable cuisines.

Vernazza (p83)

Top Sights

Musei di Strada Nuova

Genoa's trio of grand palaces. **p32**

Palazzo Reale

Genoa's most impressive palace. **p36**

Portofino

Legendary Riviera town. **p50**

Abbazia di San Fruttuoso

Medieval abbey amid breathtaking coastline. **p52**

Convento dei Cappuccini

Art-filled church overlooking
Monterosso. **p68**

Vernazza Harbour

Cinque Terre's most photogenic
waterfront. **p84**

Sentiero Azzurro –
Monterosso to Vernazza

Amazing walk along the coast. **p78**

Aquatic Adventures

Boating, kayaking, beaches and
islands. **p94**

Sentiero Azzurro – Vernazza to Corniglia

Hike amid stunning scenery. **p98**

Porto Venere

Seaside village that captivated poets. **p136**

Sentiero Rosso – Alta Via delle Cinque Terre

Trek high above Cinque Terre. **p130**

Tellaro

Charming escape from the crowds. **p140**

Eating

Surprisingly, given its lack of obvious agricultural land, the Italian Riviera is renowned for its food: fat anchovies, fragrant lemons, olive-oil-rich focaccia bread and a viridian sauce bequeathed to the world called pesto. Farming is carried out on ingeniously terraced cliff faces, and impossibly sited fishing villages have long plundered the sea.

Street Food

You can find many versions of focaccia, including the classic (called *'alla genovese'*), a simple oven-baked flatbread topped with salt and olive oil, and *focaccia col formaggio*, made with a mild creamy cheese. There's also *sardenara*, a pizza-like focaccia topped with tomatoes, onions, capers and sardines. Other top street snacks: paper cones filled with small fried fish, calamari, octopus or chips; sandwiches stuffed with ham, cheese or fish; and gelato and granita (a crushed-ice drink that is made with fruit).

Picnic Fare

The food shops are small in Cinque Terre, but with a discerning eye, you can assemble all the essentials for a memorable picnic. Start off at the antipasti counter, where you'll find cheeses, cured meats, olives, marinated seafood salads and other delicacies. Pick up some fresh fruit, bread and wine, then take it to a lovely spot out of town, in the hills or along the waterfront.

Best Ligurian

Trattoria dal Billy Serves up some of the best cooking in Cinque Terre. (pictured; p117)

Da Eraldo An atmospheric, family-friendly restaurant tucked in Monterosso's back lanes. (p74)

Osteria di Vico Palla Unfussy but mouthwatering home-cooking from a hidden restaurant near Genoa's harbour. (p44)

Trattoria Rosmarino Vibrant, incredibly popular trattoria tucked along one of Genoa's *caruggi* (narrow streets). (p44)

DANITA DELIMONT / ALAMY STOCK PHOTO ©

Best Seafood

Da Aristide Elegant but easygoing gem in Manarola with great seafood. (p117)

Trattoria da Oscar A tiny restaurant in Monterosso, with a small menu of outstanding dishes. (p74)

Gianni Franzi Have a seafood feast on Vernazza's lovely harbour front at this long-running classic. (p90)

Belforte High-end cuisine served in a medieval tower in Vernazza. (p89)

Best Street Food

Il Massimo della Focaccia Grab some focaccia for a seaside stroll in Monterosso. (p73)

Il Pescato Cucinato Order a cone of fried seafood and take it to Riomaggiore's waterfront. (p128)

Alberto Gelateria Gelato made from garden-sourced ingredients in Corniglia. (p107)

La Pia Centenaria Famed La Spezia spot firing up delicious *farinata* (chickpea-flour flatbread) for more than 130 years. (p145)

Pesto Genovese

It would be criminal to come to Genoa and not try *pesto genovese*. The city's famous pasta sauce – a pounded mix of basil, pine nuts, olive oil and sometimes garlic – really does taste, and look, better here than anywhere else, a result of the basil that's used (the leaves of very young plants are plucked daily from hothouses on city hillsides), as well as techniques honed through generations.

Drinking & Nightlife

OMERSUKRUGOKSU / GETTY IMAGES ©

Food-centric wine bars, terrace cafes with sweeping coastal views and small candlelit cocktail dens are among the draws of the drinking scene on the Italian Riviera. While nightlife is fairly limited in Cinque Terre, Genoa has a dynamic array of lively brewpubs and party spaces. La Spezia's historic centre is also sprinkled with wine bars and alfresco cafes.

Pre-Dinner Drinks

The Italian Riviera has a lively *aperitivo* scene. Starting around 5pm, the bars around village squares and pedestrianised parts of Genoa and La Spezia fill with garrulous crowds enjoying a pre-dinner alfresco drink while watching the passing people parade. A refreshing cocktail – like a *spritz* – is the drink of choice, and it goes down nicely with the complimentary snacks (olives, chips, mini *panini*, focaccia and the like) that often accompany the drinks.

Wines of Cinque Terre

Steep, terraced vineyards surround many of the villages of Cinque Terre and extend high up into the hinterlands. The wines produced in this challenging terrain were once of average quality, though things have improved remarkably in the last few years, with a new generation of winemakers returning to the land. Cinque Terre is best known for its white wines, with the native Bosco grape typically blended with Albarola and Vermentino.

Best Atmosphere

La Cantina dello Zio Bramante A fun local gathering place in Manarola with occasional live music. (p118)

Vertical Bar Buzzing spot for a cocktail in Riomaggiore at any time of day. (p129)

Les Rouges Beautifully made cocktails served under a frescoed ceiling inside a grand *palazzo*. (p46)

Malkovich A Genoese original with wildly imaginative libations enjoyed only if you know the password. (p46)

Resilience Cafe A vintage-filled classic in La Spezia. (p145)

CAROL BARRINGTON / ALAMY STOCK PHOTO ©

Best Wine Bars

Cantine Matteotti A small jewel box of a wine bar in the heart of Genoa's historic quarter. (p45)

A Piè de Campu Top-quality wines and snacks run by a knowledgeable sommelier in Manarola. (p118)

Enoteca Internazionale Get a primer on the DOC wines of Cinque Terre on Monterosso's main street. (p76)

Enoteca da Eliseo It's all about the wine at this peaceful indoor-outdoor wine bar in Monterosso. (pictured; p76)

Enoteca Il Pirun Old-time charmer in Corniglia where you can drink straight from a wine spout. (p109)

Best Drinks with a View

A Pié de Mà Unrivalled spot for a sundowner perched over the wave-kissed shores of Riomaggiore. (p129)

La Scuna Take in the views from eagle's-nest heights at this laid-back drinking spot in Corniglia. (p108)

Nessun Dorma An open-air bar with fabulous views over Manarola; go early to avoid the queues. (p118)

Bar la Marina The perfect spot for a waterfront *aperitivo* in picturesque Tellaro. (p141)

Top Winemakers

Labels to look for include Prima Terra (produced by renowned winemaker Walter de Battè), Vétua (grown just outside of Vernazza) and Tobiolo (a Manarola vineyard). Unique to Cinque Terre is the celebrated Sciacchetrà, an amber-yellow dessert wine sold in 375mL bottles.

Shopping

Genoa is the best place in the Italian Riviera for a shopping-lover's holiday. In the Cinque Terre and other small villages, souvenir stands sell much of the same-same, though you can find some unique objects, including locally made ceramics and jewellery, paintings by Ligurian artists, and speciality products (like the dessert wine, Sciacchetrà) rarely available elsewhere.

Arts & Crafts

Local artisans ply their wares at shops throughout Cinque Terre. Things to look out for include colourful jewellery – such as Bottega d'Arte's pieces that incorporate vintage elements sourced from Italian markets – and artfully designed ceramics produced by a family-run outfit in Monterosso. Artwork makes a memorable souvenir, and local painters create works showcasing the beauty of this rugged coastline.

Lemon Love

Cinque Terre's rocky soil proves to be the perfect setting to grow big juicy lemons. These are put to fine use in the region's signature tipple *limoncino* (a potent lemon liqueur). The handsome bottles, some of which are hand-painted, make great gift ideas. Lemons are also used to make fragrant soaps and pasta mixes, which are sold in abundance at shops throughout Cinque Terre. And lemon gelato is one of the great delicacies

of the region – sold at every gelateria in the area.

Best Arts & Crafts

Fabbrica d'Arte Monterosso Handsomely crafted ceramics and hand-printed linen products. (p76)

L'Emporio Paintings of marine life scenes on fragments of old fishing boats, plus the usual assortment of T-shirts and other souvenirs. (p119)

Bottega d'Arte Landscape and seascape paintings, as well as one-of-a-kind jewellery. (p93)

ANDREA IZZOTTI / SHUTTERSTOCK ©

Best Clothing & Accessories

Lanapo Beautifully made sandals by a local designer in Monterosso. (p77)

Gocce di Byron Vernazza shop selling fragrances inspired by the surrounding coasts, vineyards and forests. (p92)

Il Talismano Leather bags made in Italy and jewellery sourced from North Africa, Southern Asia and beyond. (p93)

Explora Gather essential gear (sports-tech T-shirts, walking shoes, maps) before hitting the trails. (p118)

Best Food & Drink

Enoteca Sciacchetrà Pick up a fine bottle of DOC Cinque Terre wine or delectable dessert wine in Vernazza. (p93)

Enoteca d'uu Scintu Pesto, *limoncino*, wines, olive oils and other fare. (p129)

Mercato Orientale Genova A bustling market in Genoa where you can browse for fresh fare, with delicious food counters nearby. (pictured; p44)

Best Design

Temide Fun shop in Genoa where you can look for unique gift ideas. (p47)

Via Garibaldi 12 Set in a *palazzo* on Genoa's loveliest street, this is a must for design lovers. (p47)

Hiking

CHRISTIAN MUELLER / SHUTTERSTOCK ©

Cinque Terre has a whole network of spectacular trails and you can plan some fabulous half- or full-day outings by choosing from any of 30 numbered paths. You'll also find many other trails beyond Cinque Terre, including hikes in the hillsides above Genoa and magnificent walks on the Portofino Peninsula.

Sentiero Azzurro

Sentiero Azzurro (Blue Trail; marked SVA on maps), a 12km old mule path that once linked all five oceanside villages by foot, is Cinque Terre's showcase hike, narrow and precipitous. Owing to bad storms and landslides in years past, only two sections of the trail remain open: from Monterosso to Vernazza and Vernazza to Corniglia.

Sanctuary Walks

Each of Cinque Terre's villages is associated with a sanctuary perched high on the cliffsides above the azure Mediterranean. Reaching these religious retreats used to be part of a hefty Catholic penance, but these days the walks through terraced vineyards and across view-splayed cliffs are a heavenly reward in themselves.

Best Hikes in Cinque Terre

Alta Via delle Cinque Terre (AV5T) Hike some or all of this legendary 38km trail that runs high above the villages, from Porto Venere all the way to Levanto. (p130)

Sentiero Azzurro: Monterosso to Vernazza One of the most scenic coastal walks in the Italian Riviera. (pictured above right; p78)

Sentiero Azzurro: Vernazza to Corniglia Marvel at the dramatic coastline as you walk from a waterfront piazza to a hilltop village atop a steep cliff. (p98)

MATTHIAS SCHOLZ / ALAMY STOCK PHOTO ©

Manarola to Corniglia Pass through steeply terraced vineyards en route to high-up Volastra before dropping into Cinque Terre's smallest village. (p120)

Levanto to Monterosso Visit the ruins of a medieval monastery, and gape at all five Cinque Terre Villages from atop Punta Mesco. (p64)

Santuario della Madonna delle Grazie See a much revered image of the Virgin Mary on this hour-long walk (one way that is) up above Vernazza. (p107)

Santuario della Madonna di Soviore Check out an impressive church and recharge over homemade cakes at this sanctuary above Monterosso. (p74)

Best Hikes Outside of Cinque Terre

Palmaria Catch a ferry to this island off Porto Venere for a walk without the crowds, then finish with a dip in the sea. (p97)

Portesone Take trail 431 from Tellaro to visit the ruins of a village abandoned during a plague epidemic. (p141)

Parco Naturale Regionale di Portofino Hike from Camogli to the seaside monastery of San Fruttuoso over a lushly forested peninsula. (p51)

Hiking Resources

Parco Nazionale Cinque Terre (www.parconazionale5terre.it) Get hiking details and the most up-to-date trail information.

Parco di Portofino (www.parcoportofino.com) The lowdown on the 80km of trails on the Portofino peninsula.

Lerici Coast (www.lericicoast.it) Maps and route info on walks near Lerici, San Terenzo and Tellaro.

For Kids

Cinque Terre and the Italian Riviera has endless appeal for young travellers. This is a land of seaside fun on the beach, scenic boat rides and enjoyable hikes for older kids, with rewarding snacks (focaccia, gelato, pizza!) never far away. Other highlights include clambering through castle rooms in Lerici, riding a cable car high above Rapallo and going eye-to-eye with Mediterranean marine creatures in Genoa's aquarium.

Beaches & Swimming Spots

Monterosso has a long pebbly beach that makes for a great day out without leaving Cinque Terre. There are also small beaches in Vernazza and Riomaggiore. Further afield, you can find some enchanting stretches of shoreline in Levanto, Sestri Levante, Lerici and San Terenzo. Kids don't always need a beach for aquatic fun. On calm days, kids who know how to swim can take a dip in the pool-like spot off Manarola's marina or jump into the waters off the dock below Corniglia.

Fun in Genoa

While many travellers breeze through this port city, there are some appealing attractions for children. Down on the revitalised waterfront, you'll find one of Europe's largest aquariums, a rotating platform with grand views and departing boat trips with dolphin-watching opportunities.

Best Beaches

San Terenzo Enjoy the (usually) calm waters of this beach just north of Lerici. (pictured; p139)

Punta Chiappa Catch a boat or hike from Camogli to this pretty seaside spot. (p57)

Sestri Levante Frolick in the waves just off this picturesque town a short train ride from Cinque Terre. (p60)

Levanto Walk the beachfront in this pretty town near Cinque Terre or take a bike ride along the promenade. (p62)

Monterosso Play in the water just a short stroll from Monterosso's train station. (p67)

POLUDZIBER / SHUTTERSTOCK ©

Best Rainy-Day Activities

Palazzo Reale Check out the Hall of Mirrors inside this former royal residence. (p36)

Acquario Gaze at amazing undersea wonders inside Genoa's impressive aquarium. (p42)

Museo Tecnico Navale della Spezia See model ships and fantastical figureheads in La Spezia's naval museum. (p143)

Best Adventures

Centro Visito Batterie Silvio Sommazzi Clamber around the remnants of WWII bunkers while hiking the trails of the Portofino peninsula. (p20)

Ferrovia Genova Casella Marvel at the views of old forts while riding this narrow-gauge railway from Genoa to Casella. (p45)

Sentiero Azzurro: Monterosso to Vernazza Hiking a coastal trail, with gelato and other treats awaiting at the end. (p78)

Tours

Guided walking tours are a great way to get beneath the surface, learning about the culture, cuisine and history that have shaped this fascinating corner of Italy. For something more adventurous, you can head off on a guided kayaking trip, go rock climbing with a pro, take a scenic boat tour, or see the underside of the Italian Riviera coast on a diving excursion.

YULIA GRIGORYEVA / SHUTTERSTOCK ©

Arbaspàa (☏0187 76 00 83; www.arbaspaa.com; Via Discovolo 252; 👣) Manarola agency offering a vast range of activities, including wine-tasting at a local vineyard, boat trips, kayaking excursions, photography tours, hiking trips and more.

Crazy Boat Cinque Terre (☏328 9365595; www.crazyboatcinqueterre. com; boat hire per hour €100) Create a customised boat tour, stopping for a swim off Guvano Beach, checking out the waterfall near Monterosso or making a sunset cruise.

Diving Center 5 Terre (☏0187 92 00 11; www.5terrediving.it; Via San Giacomo; dive/snorkel excursion per person €60/20; ⏱10am-4pm Apr-Oct) Riomaggiore outfit that runs dives and snorkelling excursions.

Whale Watch Liguria (☏010 26 57 12; www. whalewatchliguria.it; Ponte Spinola; adult/child €35/20; ⏱1pm Tue & 2pm Sat May-early Oct) These five-hour spring and summer tours from Genoa offer fascinating insight on the world's largest mammals.

Zenaverde Bike Tours (☏010 455 03 78; www. zenaverde.com; 1/3hr tours per person from €50/75) Tour Genoa's historic centre on an electric bike, or head up into the hills or to nearby coastal towns.

Centro Visito Batterie Silvio Sommazzi (☏348 0182556; www.par coportofino.com; Chiappa; guided tours adult/child €5/3; ⏱10am-5pm Sat & Sun Mar–mid-Jun & Sep) Runs one-hour tours of the military post (pictured) in the hills outside Camogli. Also offers longer tours of other parts of the peninsula.

Wine Tasting & Culinary Courses

Guided wine tasting is available in Cinque Terre, and you can also visit the terraced vineyards on a tour departing from several of the villages. There's also tutorials on making pesto (one of the Riviera's great gifts to Italian cooking) and creating your own pasta from scratch.

LOOK / ALAMY STOCK PHOTO ©

A Piè de Campu (☎338 2220088; apiedecampu@ gmail.com; Via Discovolo; wine tasting €30-50, vineyard tour from €50) Offers guided wine tastings in Manarola led by a deeply knowledgeable sommelier. You can also book pesto-making and pasta-making courses, or go on a vineyard (and tasting) tour.

Cantina Nessun Dorma (www.nessundormacinque terre.com; Piazza Papa Innocenzo IV; ☉2-8pm Wed-Mon, to 10pm Jul & Aug, closed Nov-Feb) The best place in Manarola to learn about (and more importantly tasting!) the

wines of Cinque Terre. The tiny shop sells bottles and wines by the glass, and also offers wine tastings led by extremely knowledgeable staff.

Vernazza Winexperience (Deck Giani Franzi; ☎331 3433801; www. vernazzawinexperience.com; Via San Giovanni Battista 41; wine tasting from €15; ☉5-9pm Apr-Oct) Sommelier Alessandro Villa's family have lived in Vernazza for over six generations. Let him take you through the rare, small-yield wines that come from the vineyards that tumble down the surrounding hills.

Cantina Cinque Terre Enjoy tasting dry white wines and Sciacchetrà after a vineyard tour at Cinque Terre's largest wine producer, situated near Manarola. (p116)

Buranco (☎0187 817 677; www.burancocinqueterre. it; Via Buranco 72; ☉noon-6pm by advanced booking) Near Monterosso, Buranco is a verdant oasis that produces some fine DOC Cinque Terre white wines as well as grappa, *limoncino,* and the dessert wine Sciacchetrà. Before or after a tasting on the verandah, you can wander the terraced vineyards.

Four Perfect Days

Day 1

ANDREJ PRIVIZER / SHUTTERSTOCK ©

Day 2

BRZOZOWSKA / GETTY IMAGES ©

Spend the first day exploring Genoa's historic centre. Marvel at the grandeur of the palaces of the **Musei di Strada Nuova** (p32), then take a stroll along the photogenic waterfront.

Have a pesto-accented lunch at local favourite **Trattoria da Maria** (p45), then get lost in Genoa's atmospheric *caruggi* (narrow lanes). Be sure to stop by Gothic treasures like the **Cattedrale di San Lorenzo** (pictured; p42) and the **Chiesa del Gesù** (p43).

In the late afternoon, have an *aperitivo* amid the frescoes of **Les Rouges** (p46), then head to **Trattoria Rosmarino** (p44) for down-home Ligurian classics. End the evening with a creative cocktail in the speakeasy-style bar of **Malkovich** (p46).

Catch an early train to the pretty seaside village of **Camogli** (p55). Hit the trail early for the scenic walk through forest and along sea cliffs to the **Abbazia di San Fruttuoso** (p52), a medieval abbey perched on the shoreline.

After lazing on the beach and having a picnic, catch an onward boat to **Portofino** (pictured; p50). Stroll out to the lighthouse, go window shopping on the elegant lanes and enjoy drinks by the harbour. Later catch a boat to Santa Margherita and a train back to Camogli.

Have a seafood dinner at **Da Paolo** (p56), followed by an evening stroll along Camogli's pretty waterfront. **La Mancina** (p57) makes a fine spot for a nightcap.

Day 3

Take a morning train to Monterosso. Stroll through the old lanes, watch village life from a cafe and pick up snacks for the day ahead, then hike to Vernazza along the lovely **Sentiero Azzurro** (p78).

Have lunch in Vernazza at harbourside **Gianni Franzi** (p90), then browse for gifts and souvenirs along Via Roma. If you're not exhausted, continue on foot on the **Sentiero Azzurro** (p98) to Corniglia. Otherwise take the train one stop.

Stroll Corniglia, stopping for an afternoon treat at **Alberto Gelateria** (p107), and sea gazing at the cliffside **Belvedere di Santa Maria** (p109). Train it back to Monterosso before sunset for drinks at **Torre Aurora** (pictured; p73) followed by dinner at **Da Eraldo** (p74).

Day 4

Start day four in Riomaggiore. Wander up above town for sweeping coastal views, then browse the snack stands for some Ligurian treats – which you can enjoy down on pretty **Fossola Beach** (p127).

Afterwards, have a pick-me-up on the seaside terrace of **A Pié de Mà** (p129). Then take the train one stop to Manarola.

Walk up to **Punta Bonfiglio** (p115) for a magical view over town, have an afternoon drink at **Nessun Dorma** (pictured; p118), then end the Cinque Terre experience with a fabulous meal at **Trattoria dal Billy** (p117). If you're not ready to call it a night, join the festivities at **La Cantina dello Zio Bramante** (p118).

Need to Know

For detailed information, see Survival Guide (p147)

Currency
Euro (€)

Language
Italian

Visas
Generally not required for stays of up to 90 days (or at all by EU nationals). Some nationalities will need a Schengen visa.

Money
ATMs are widespread in Italy. Major credit cards are widely accepted, but some smaller shops, trattorias and hotels might not take them.

Mobile Phones
Local SIM cards can be used in European, Australian and some unlocked US phones.

Time
Central European Time (GMT/UTC plus one hour)

Tipping
Italians are not big tippers, and service is usually included in the restaurant bill.

Daily Budget

Budget: Less than €110

Dorm bed: €23–30

Double room in a budget hotel: €60–100

Focaccia slice: €2.50

Set lunch menu: €10–12

Train ticket within Cinque Terre: €4

Midrange: €110–200

Double room in a hotel: €170–200

Meal at a trattoria: €20–40

Admission to Genoa museums: €8

Ferry from Camogli to Portofino: €11

Bottle of *limoncino:* €12

Top End: More than €200

Boutique hotel room: €190–450

Seafood dinner: €45–60

Two-hour private boat excursion: €200

Cocktails: €9

Advance Planning

Three months before Book accommodation, particularly if visiting during the high season (June through early September). Ensure your passport is up to date.

One week before Book tables at top restaurants. Reach out to tour operators like Arbaspàa and reserve outdoor activities, vineyard tours and other excursions.

A few days before Check the weather forecast on the Riviera and prepare accordingly. Add useful apps like Google Translate and Trenitalia (Italy's rail network) to your phone.

Arriving in Genoa & Cinque Terre

✈ Cristoforo Colombo Airport

From Cristoforo Colombo Airport, the **Volabus** (📞 848 000030; www.amt.genova.it; one way €6) runs to/from Genoa's two main train stations (Piazza Principe and Brignole) at least hourly between 5.50am to 12.20am from the airport. A taxi to the centre costs €20 to €30.

⚓ Porto Antico Ferry Terminal

Golfo Paradiso SNC (📞 392 1375558; www.golfoparadiso.it) operates boats to Camogli (one way/return €10/17), Portofino (€15/24) and Cinque Terre (€21/38).

🚉 Train Stations

Genoa's Stazione Principe and Stazione Brignole are linked by frequent trains to Milan, Pisa, Rome and Turin.

Getting Around

🚆 Train

There is good train service between Genoa and La Spezia, with stops at Camogli, Santa Margherita Ligure, Sestri Levante, Levanto and the Cinque Terre villages.

🚌 Bus

Villages that lack train stations are connected to nearby rail hubs. Buses from La Spezia go to Porto Venere, San Terenzo and Lerici. Buses to Portofino go from Santa Margherita Ligure. Trips take 30 minutes.

🚶 Walk

A trail network connects neighbouring villages on the Ligurian coast.

⚓ Ferry

Ferries operated by **Servizio Marittimo del Tigullio** (www.traghettiportofino.it) connect Santa Margherita Ligure with Cinque Terre, Porto Venere, Portofino and Rapallo.

Stazione Brignole, Genoa

Genoa & Cinque Terre Regions

Cristoforo
Colombo

Genoa (p31)
The once mighty maritime capital is packed with palaces, grand squares, and an historic centre famed for its *caruggi* (narrow lanes).

• Camogli   •Rapallo

•Santa Margherita
Ligure

*Abbazia
di San
Fruttuoso*   ◉ *Portofino*

• Sestri
Levant

Portofino Peninsula to Levanto (p49)
East of Genoa lies coastal enclaves, photogenic beaches and a peninsula covered in forested walking trails.

Vernazza (p83)
The Riviera's most photographed village has a mesmerising harbour fringed by pastel-hued buildings. A memorable trail connects Vernazza with both Monterosso and Corniglia.

Corniglia (p103)
Perched on a rocky promontory, this tiny settlement has obvious appeal, particularly when strolling Corniglia's main street with its eclectic shops and eateries

Monterosso (p67)

Cinque Terre's westernmost village has a long beach, a hilltop church and well-positioned restaurants overlooking the dramatic shoreline.

La Spezia & the Bay of Poets (p135)

A short hop east of Riomaggiore is the vibrant city of La Spezia and a picturesque bay ringed by captivating towns.

Levanto

Lerici

Tellaro

Porto Venere

Manarola (p111)

Backed by terraced vineyards, Manarola offers magnificent views from the trails above town, and some fine spots for indulging in wine and seafood

Riomaggiore (p123)

The biggest village of the Cinque Terre has intriguing medieval buildings and a rocky beach overlooking crystalline waters just outside the village.

Explore
Genoa & Cinque Terre

Manarola (p111) JULIA LAV / SHUTTERSTOCK ©

Explore

Genoa

Italy's largest sea port is indefatigably contradictory, full at once of grandeur, squalor, sparkling light and deep shade. A gateway to the Riviera for many travellers, Genoa is famed for its extensive old city, with its atmospheric medieval lanes, splendid palaces, and grand plazas bursting with civic life. While still under the tourism radar, Genoa is a fabulous city to explore.

The Short List

○ **Musei di Strada Nuova (p32)** *Wandering one of Italy's most beautiful baroque streets and discovering each palazzo's treasures.*

○ **Old City (p38)** *Exploring the atmospheric caruggi (narrow streets) of Genoa's fabulously intact medieval heart.*

○ **Funicolare Zecca-Righi (p45)** *Riding this funicular up to leafy hillsides and hiking out to the old forts that once guarded Genoa.*

○ **Via Garibaldi 12 (p47)** *Browsing the high-design wares in what just might be Italy's most beautiful shop.*

○ **Les Rouges (p46)** *Sipping bespoke cocktails and nibbling on creative appetizers under frescoed ceilings.*

Getting There & Around

✈ Domestic and international services, including Ryanair, use Cristoforo Colombo Airport, 6km west of the city.

⚓ Ferries connect Genoa's Porto Antico with Camogli, Portofino, Cinque Terre and other Riviera destinations.

Ⓜ Genoa has a handy eight-station metro line.

🚇 Genoa's Stazione Principe and Stazione Brignole are linked by very frequent trains to Milan, Pisa, Rome and Turin.

Genoa Map on p40

Piazza de Ferrari (p39) ROMAN SIGAEV / SHUTTERSTOCK ©

Top Sight
Musei di Strada Nuova

Skirting the northern edge of the old city limits, pedestrianised Via Garibaldi was planned by Galeazzo Alessi in the 16th century. It quickly became the most sought-after quarter, lined with the palaces of Genoa's wealthiest citizens. Three of these palazzi – Rosso, Bianco and Doria-Tursi – today comprise the Musei di Strada Nuova. Between them, they hold the city's finest collection of old masters.

◎ MAP P40, E3

Palazzi dei Rolli

www.museidigenova.it

Via Garibaldi

adult/reduced €9/7

🕘 9am-7pm Tue-Fri, 10am-7.30pm Sat & Sun Apr-Sep, 9.30am-6.30pm Oct-Mar

Palazzo Rosso

Named after the rich red (*rosso*) hue of the facade, Palazzo Rosso (pictured) is the most atmospheric of the bunch, and not to be missed. Lavishly frescoed rooms set with decorative art and period furniture provide the backdrop to fine works by Van Dyck, Veronese, Dürer and Strozzi, among many other European masters. There is also some surprising architecture and design on display, as well as an artfully designed courtyard and a viewing platform on the rooftop.

Frescoes

The 2nd floor is awash with frescoes painted by some of the Italian Riviera's greatest 17th-century artists. Standouts include the four successive rooms depicting the allegory of the seasons, painted by Gregorio de Ferrari (spring and summer) and Domenico Piola (autumn and winter). *Loggia delle Rovine* (Ruins of the Loggia) is a wonderful work of *trompe l'œil*, which places the myth of Diana and Endymion in the ruins of a classical mansion.

Paintings

The wealthy noble Gio Francesco Brignole commissioned Van Dyck – one of the greatest artists of his time – to paint full-length portraits of his family members in 1627. These exquisite works would later hang in the family home of Palazzo Rosso, where they remain today. They are joined by other Van Dyck masterpieces, including *Christ Carrying the Cross* and *Portrait of a Gentleman of the Spinola Family*. Other standouts include Guido Reni's *San Sebastiano* and Guercino's *La morte di Cleopatra* (The Death of Cleopatra), as well as the lifelike *Pifferaio* (Flute Player) by Bernardo Strozzi and Veronese's macabre *Judith and Holofernes*.

The Albini Apartments

The 3rd floor of Palazzo Rosso hides an Italian mid-century gem – an apartment designed by architect Franco Albini (1905–77) for the

---

★ **Top Tips**

○ Go right at opening time to beat the crowds. Start with the blockbuster of the three – Palazzo Rosso.

○ You get free admission to the Musei di Strada Nuova at the end of the historic centre walking tour offered by Genoa's tourist office.

○ After visiting the *palazzi*, be sure to check out the other grand buildings on this street. Some have courtyards that are open to the public.

✕ **Take a Break**

Get your daily gelato infusion a short walk from Via Garibaldi at the excellent **Gelateria Profumo** (www.villa1827.it; Vico Superiore del Ferro 14; cones from €2.50; ⏱ noon-7.30pm Tue-Sat).

Pick up a slice of focaccia and other freshly baked goodies at **Pane e Tulipani** (☎ 010 817 88 41; Via dei Macelli di Soziglia 75; snacks from €2; ⏱ 6am-7.30pm Mon-Sat).

museum's director. Its mix of signature Albini furniture, clean modern lines and Genoese excess, will delight design fans (the city views aren't bad either). One of Italy's best-loved 20th-century architects, Albini was a key figure in the restoration of Genoa's *palazzi* in the post-war period.

Palazzo Bianco

Flemish, Spanish and Italian artists feature at Palazzo Bianco, the second of the triumvirate of *palazzi*. Rubens' sensual and lushly painted *Venere e Marte* (Venus and Mars) and Van Dyck's *Vertumno e Pomona* – painted during his Genoese period – dominate room 18. Other splendid works showcase the talents of Hans Memling, Filippino Lippi and Murillo. There's also an assortment of 15th-century religious icons.

Courtyards

The palace has several elegant courtyards spread across two different levels. The first, accessed from the 1st floor of the museum, maintains its 18th-century design, complete with cobblestone mosaic paths, fountains and ornamental gardens. The second courtyard – reached on the pathway to Palazzo Doria-Tursi – contains the remains of a once impressive Gothic church. From here, you'll continue on into the galleries of Palazzo Doria-Tursi (no need to exit back onto the street).

Textile Collections

On the mezzanine floor, Palazzo Bianco's textile collections hold a trove of men's and women's fashion

Palazzo Bianco

from several centuries. Garments here hail from across the globe, and include elaborate Kashmir shawls, 19th-century dresses of the Ottoman Empire, 18th-century French Argentan laces, and finely embroidered silks and gala costumes of the Napoleonic era.

Palazzo Doria-Tursi

Boasting a grand facade of marble, sandstone and slate, Palazzo Doria-Tursi was built in the late 16th century for Nicolò Grimaldi, who had deep ties to royalty. It later passed to Giovanni Andrea Doria, prince of Melfi, who enhanced the edifice with hanging gardens and side galleries. He also assembled a collection of tapestries and artworks from England and Flanders. In the 19th century, the palace saw more transformations – including the adding of the clock turret – under the ownership of Vittorio Emanuele I of Savoy. In the second half of the 19th century, the halls were decorated with frescoes.

Sala degli Arazzi

The aptly named Sala degli Arazzi (Hall of Tapestries) displays an impressive collection of textile art. It was assembled in part thanks to the close economic ties Genoa had with Flanders dating back to the 14th century. Among the treasures are several fine Flemish tapestries depicting events from the life of Alexander the Great.

Sala Paganini

The final rooms feature a small but absorbing collection of legendary violinist Niccolò Paganini's personal effects. Pride of place goes to the great musician's Cannone violin, made in Cremona in 1743. One lucky musician gets to play the maestro's violin during October's Paganini festival. Other artefacts on show include letters, musical scores and his travelling chess set. Enter the galleries via Palazzo Bianco.

Town Hall

In addition to fine art and priceless musical instruments, the palace also houses Genoa's town hall – a role it's held since 1848. There's no charge to wander around the courtyard and admire the design from the staircases (simply enter via the main palace entrance at no 9).

Top Sight 📷
Palazzo Reale

If you only get the chance to visit one of the Palazzi dei Rolli (group of palaces belonging to the city's most eminent families), make it this one. A former residence of the Savoy dynasty, it has terraced gardens, exquisite furnishings, a fine collection of 17th-century art and a gilded Hall of Mirrors that is worth the entry fee alone.

◎ MAP P40, B1

☏ 010 271 02 36

www.palazzorealegenova.beniculturali.it

Via Balbi 10

adult/reduced €6/2

⏱ 9am-2pm Tue & Fri, 9am-7pm Wed & Thu, 1.30-7pm Sat & Sun

History of the Palace

The palace was built by the wealthy Balbi family in the 1640s but went through various transformations as the Durazzo family bought the building in 1679 and redecorated many of the rooms, redesigned the facade on Via Balbi and rebuilt the Teatro del Falcone. Renovations of the early 18th century added some of the *palazzo's* most dramatic features. Hard times forced the Durazzos to sell the building, which ultimately became a royal palace after it was purchased by Vittorio Emanuele I, King of Sardinia, in 1824. The Emanuele clan renovated various rooms, creating a throne room, audience chamber and ballroom among other refitting. It remained a royal residence until 1919, when King Vittorio Emanuele III ceded it to the Italian State.

The Layout

The grandeur of this noble residence is apparent as you ascend the stairs and wander through a series of elaborately decorated rooms. Through these photogenic chambers you'll find a mix of oversized oil paintings, lavish stucco details, classical marble sculptures, Flemish tapestries and dazzling ceiling frescoes. Highlights include the Hall of Mirrors, designed by Domenico Parodi in the 1720s and 1730s. Influenced by the Galerie des Glaces in Versailles, the staggering room is lined with exquisitely carved statues of Roman deities, like *Adonis,* a 17th-century work by Filippo Parodi – the greatest Genoese sculptor of his time. Further along, the King's Bedroom features frescoes by Tommaso Aldrovandini and the palace's greatest treasure – the painting *Cristo spirante* (Christ Crucified) by Van Dyck.

★ **Top Tips**

o To see the royal apartments, you'll have to plan carefully. The 1st floor opens only on Saturday mornings (9am to 1.30pm) and during special exhibitions.

o If you plan to visit Musei di Strada Nuova and other sites around Genoa, it's worth investing in the Card Musei di Genova, which gives access to over 20 museums and palaces around the city. It costs €12 for 24 hours (€20 for 48 hours).

✕ **Take a Break**

La Focacceria di Teobaldo (Via Balbi 115; focaccia from €2.50; 🕙8am-7pm Mon-Sat) serves up tasty focaccia slices just a short stroll up Via Balbi from the museum.

Pizzeria Savô (p44) serves outstanding pizzas with both classical and unusual varieties. It's tucked along a narrow lane about an eight-minute walk southeast of the museum.

Walking Tour 🥾

Historic Genoa

On this photogenic stroll through Genoa's old quarter, you'll take in fresco-covered buildings, stately plazas and imposing entrance gates that date back to the Middle Ages. The contrasts are dramatic – after winding through the caruggi (narrow lanes), you'll get an eyeful of palaces along Via Garibaldi, followed by a lofty panorama from a hilltop overlook.

Walk Facts

Start Palazzo San Giorgio;
Ⓜ San Giorgio

End Spianata Castelletto;
Ⓜ Darsena

Length 3km; two hours

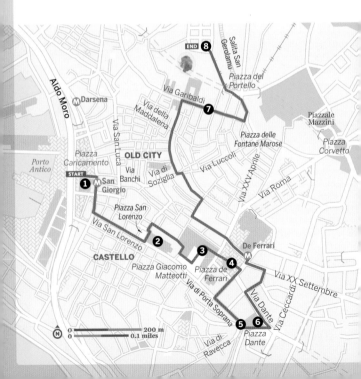

❶ Palazzo San Giorgio

Begin on the waterfront facing the **Palazzo San Giorgio**. Built in 1260, this striking palace has frescoes depicting some of Genoa's hometown heroes, including Christopher Columbus (second from the right). It was also the birthplace of Genoa's first bank, which opened here in 1407.

❷ Cattedrale di San Lorenzo

Walk around the building and head into the narrow lanes of the old town, continuing up Via San Lorenzo to the **Cattedrale di San Lorenzo** (p42). This iconic black-and-white cathedral dates back to the 1100s, and was once the epicentre of medieval Genoa.

❸ Palazzo Ducale

Follow the dark alleys around the church to reach the grand **Palazzo Ducale** (www.palazzoducale.genova.it; Piazza Giacomo Matteotti 9; price varies by exhibition; ☺hours vary). The palace, first built in 1298, was once the Doge's residence and became a symbol of Genoese power. Head inside for a look at the atrium.

❹ Piazza de Ferrari

Exit the other side of the *palazzo* onto the photogenic **Piazza de Ferrari**. Set with a circular fountain the plaza is ringed by majestic buildings, including the Palazzo della Borsa (the former stock exchange), a masterpiece of Genoese art nouveau.

❺ Porta Soprana

Exit the plaza on the south side and turn left at the end of the street. Ahead lies the imposing **Porta Soprana**. This towering entrance gate, erected in the 12th century, was once part of the city's substantial defences.

❻ Casa di Colombo

Stroll through the old stonework and take the narrow lane, which leads past the ruins of a Romanesque cloister. A few steps further is the **Casa di Colombo** (www. coopculture.it; Piazza Dante; adult/ child €5/3; ☺11am-5pm Tue-Sun), an 18th-century reconstruction of the house where the famed Genoese navigator Christopher Columbus once allegedly lived.

❼ Via Garibaldi

Pass back through the Piazza de Ferrari and wind your way along the *caruggi* to **Via Garibaldi**. Genoa's most lavish street is lined with grand *palazzi,* some of which date back to the 16th century. Take a peak inside No 11, the Palazzo Doria-Tursi (p35), which houses Genoa's town hall.

❽ Spianata Castelletto

Walk to the Piazza del Portello. From here take the art-nouveau *ascensore* (lift) – you can also walk up Via Salita San Gerolamu – to the **Spianata Castelletto**. As you take in the sweeping panorama from this leafy viewpoint, it's easy to see why Genoa is known as La Superba.

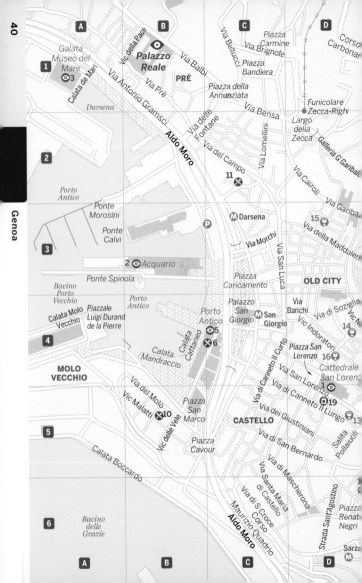

Genoa

A
B
C
D

1
Galata Museo del Mare ⊙3
Vic della Pace
⊙ Palazzo Reale
Via della Pace
Via Balbi
Via Brignole
Piazza Carmine
Corso Carbonar
Via Bellucci
Piazza Bandiera
Via Balbi
Via Pré
PRÉ
Via Antonio Gramsci
Calata de Mari

Darsena

Aldo Moro
Piazza della Annunziata
Via Bensa
Funicolare Zecca-Righi
Largo della Zecca
Galleria G Garibald
Via delle Fontane
Via del Campo
Via Lomellini
Via Cairoli
Via Gariba

2
Porto Antico

Via della Maddaler
11

3
Ponte Morosini
Ponte Calvi
P
Ⓜ Darsena
Via Morchi
15
Via San Luca

Bacino Porto Vecchio
Ponte Spinola
2 ⊙ Acquario
Piazza Caricamento
OLD CITY

4
Calata Molo Vecchio
Piazzale Luigi Durand de la Pierre
Porto Antico
Porto Antico
⊙5
✕6
Calata Cattaneo
Calata Mandraccio
Palazzo San Giorgio
Ⓜ San Giorgio
Via Banchi
Via di Sozigli
Vic Indoratori
Vic N
14
MOLO VECCHIO
Piazza San Lorenzo
16
Cattedrale San Lorenz
⊙

5
Via del Molo
Vic Malatti
✕10
Vic delle Vele
Piazza San Marco
Via di Canneto il Curto
Via San Lorenzo
Via di Canneto il Lungo
⊕19
Piazza Cavour
CASTELLO
Via dei Giustiniani
Salita Poilauoli
13

6
Calata Boccardo
Bacino delle Grazie
Via di San Bernardo
Via di Mascherona
Via Santa Maria di Castello
Corso
Maurizio Quadrio
Via di S. Croce
Strada Sant'Agostino
Piazza Renato Negri
Sarze
Ⓜ

A
B
C
D

Genoa

For reviews see

⊙	Top Sights	p32
⊙	Sights	p42
❸	Eating	p43
⊜	Drinking	p45
⊛	Entertainment	p47
⊕	Shopping	p47

E
Corso Firenze
Corso Paganini
F
Corso Paganini
Corso Magenta
G
0   200 m
0   0.1 miles
H

1

Piazza Golfredo Villa
CASTELLETTO

Via Caffaro
Via G Bertora

Salita S Gerolamu
Salita Sant'Anna

2

Musei di Strada Nuova
Piazza del Portello
Salita Battistina
Via G Mameli
Via Goito
Via Palestro
Via Assarotti

a Garibaldi 12
Galleria N Bixio
Via Piaggio
Piazzale Mazzini
Piazza Marsala
Via Pescheria

9 ❸

Piazza delle Fontane Marose
Piazza Corvetto
Via Serra

3

Via Luccoli
❸12
Spianata dell'Acquasola
Via Carcassi

Vic della Casana
20
Via XXV Aprile
Via Roma
Galleria Mazzini
Via Caba
Via XII Ottobre
Via Pammat
V IV Novembre

4

17 ⊛
Piazza Piccapietra
Piazza Portona

❸7
P
Piazza de Ferrari
Via E Vernazza
Via V Dicembre

Piazza iacomo atteotti
Piazza de Ferrari
De Ferrari

5

4⊙ Chiesa del Gesù
Via di Porta Soprana
Via Dante
Via Ceccardi
Via Fieschi
Via XX Settembre
Via San Vincenzo

ic del Fico
Via di Ravecca
Piazza Dante
Salita San Leonardo
Corso Podesta
Via d'Archi
❸8

6

Via d'Annunzio
Via I Frugoni
Via Malta
Via Maragliano
Via Fiasella
Via Cesarea

E
F
G
H

Sights

Cattedrale di San Lorenzo

CATHEDRAL

1 MAP P40, D5

Genoa's zebra-striped Gothic–Romanesque cathedral owes its continued existence to the poor quality of a British WWII bomb that failed to ignite here in 1941; it still sits on the right side of the nave like an innocuous museum piece. The cathedral, fronted by three arched portals, twisting columns and crouching lions, was first consecrated in 1118. The two bell towers and cupola were added later in the 16th century. (Piazza San Lorenzo; ☉8am-noon & 3-7pm)

Acquario

AQUARIUM

2 MAP P40, B3

Genoa's aquarium is one of the largest in Europe, with more than 600 species of sea creatures, including sharks. Moored at the end of a walkway is the ship *Grande Nave Blu*, a floating display with exhibits of coral reefs. The aquarium's 'cetaceans pavilion' may concern some visitors: while the dolphins do not perform tricks and the aquarium fulfils its international legal requirements, including rehousing abused dolphins, animal welfare groups claim keeping dolphins in enclosed tanks is harmful. (☎010 2 34 51; www.acquariodigenova.it; Ponte Spinola; adult/reduced €32/21; ☉9am-8pm Mar-Jun, Sep & Oct, 8.30am-9pm Jul & Aug, 9.30am-8pm Nov-Feb)

Chiesa del Gesù

Galata Museo del Mare

MUSEUM

3 MAP P40, A1

Genoa was rivalled only by Barcelona and Venice as a medieval and Renaissance maritime power, so its 'museum of the sea' is, not surprisingly, one of its most relevant and interesting. High-tech exhibits trace the history of seafaring, from Genoa's reign as Europe's greatest dockyard to the ages of sail and steam. (www.galatamuseodelmare.it; Calata de Mari 1; adult/child €13/8; 10am-7.30pm daily Mar-Oct, 10am-6pm Tue-Fri, to 7.30pm Sat & Sun Nov-Feb)

Chiesa del Gesù

CHURCH

4 MAP P40, E5

Hidden behind Piazza de Ferrari (p39), this former Jesuit church dating from 1597 has an intricate and lavish interior. The wonderfully frescoed walls and ceiling are anchored by two works by the great Dutch artist Rubens. *Circoncisione* (Circumcision) hangs over the main altar, and *Miracolo di San Ignazio* is displayed in a side chapel. (Piazza Giacomo Matteotti; 3.30-7.30pm Mon, 7am-1pm & 3.30-7.30pm Tue-Sat, 8am-1pm & 4-10pm Sun)

Porto Antico

AREA

5 MAP P40, C4

The port that once controlled a small empire is now one of the most popular places to enjoy a *passeggiata* (evening stroll).

Genoa's Old City

The heart of medieval Genoa – bounded by ancient city gates Porta dei Vacca and Porta Soprana, and the streets of Via Cairoli, Via Garibaldi and Via XXV Aprile – is famed for its *caruggi* (narrow lanes). Looking up at the washing pegged on lines everywhere, it becomes obvious that these dark, cave-like laneways and blind alleys are still largely residential, although the number of fashionable bars, shops and cafes continues to grow.

Superyacht lovers are particularly well catered for and those with kids will love the aquarium, the futuristic Bigo (lookout), the small public swimming pool and the pirate ship. (www.portoantico.it)

Eating

Il Marin

SEAFOOD €€€

6 MAP P40, C4

Eating by the water often means a compromise in quality, but Eataly's 3rd-floor fine-dining space delivers both panoramic port views and Genoa's most innovative seafood menu. Rustic wooden tables, Renzo Piano–blessed furniture and an open kitchen make for an easy, relaxed glamour, while dishes use unusual Mediterranean-sourced produce and look gorgeous on the plate. Book ahead. (Eataly Genova;

📞010 869 87 22; www.eataly.net;
Porto Antico; meals €50-60, eight-
course menu €75; ⏱noon-3pm &
7-10.30pm Wed-Mon)

Trattoria Rosmarino

TRATTORIA €€

7 🍴 MAP P40, E4

Rosmarino cooks up the standard
local specialities, yes, but the
straightforwardly priced menu has
an elegance and vibrancy that sets
it apart. With two nightly sittings,
there's always a nice buzz (though
there are also enough nooks and
crannies that a romantic night for
two isn't out of the question). Call
ahead for an evening table. (📞010
251 04 75; www.trattoriarosmarino.it;
Salita del Fondaco 30; meals €28-34;
⏱12.30-2.30pm & 7.30-10.30pm
Mon-Sat)

Mercato Orientale Genova

ITALIAN €

8 🍴 MAP P40, H6

In 2019 a gourmet food hall
landed in Genoa's oldest market,
offering nearly a dozen different
stands. You can dine on wood-
oven-fired pizzas, pastas, burgers,
focaccia, panini, tacos and fresh
seafood. A square bar stands at
the centre of the vast 19th-
century hall, and there's also a
wine bar and a high-end restaurant helmed by the celebrated
young chef Daniele Rebosio. (MOG;
📞010 897 30 00; www.moggenova.it;
Via XX Settembre 75; mains from €8;
⏱10am-11.45pm; 🍴)

Bella Bu

LIGURIAN €€

9 🍴 MAP P40, E3

An atmospherically lit spot for
tapas and cocktails early in the
evening, or a proper dinner later
in the night. The youthful owners showcase quality seasonal
and market-fresh ingredients in
creative plates that pull from both
Ligurian and Spanish recipes, all of
which pair nicely with the natural
wines on offer. (📞010 247 42 09;
www.bellabubistrot.com; Vico Inferiore
del Ferro 9; meals €25-40; ⏱6.30pm-
1am Mon-Thu, to 2am Fri & Sat)

Osteria di Vico Palla

LIGURIAN €€

10 🍴 MAP P40, B5

This old-fashioned tavern near
the waterfront has been around
in one form or another since the
1600s. Wooden tables, low-arched
brick ceilings and a few nautical
knick-knacks set the scene for
seafood feasting with a minimum
of fuss. The changing chalkboard
menu (brought to your table) is
replete with Genoese delicacies.
(📞010 246 65 75; www.osteriadi
vicopalla.com; Vico Palla 15; meals
€26-36; ⏱12.30-3pm & 7.30-11pm
Tue-Sun)

Pizzeria Savô

PIZZA €

11 🍴 MAP P40, C2

Gourmet pizza in Italy seems a
little, well, ironic, with the rest of
the world so keen to do authentic
Italian pizza. While the pizzas here
are undoubtedly fancy by local

Mountain Escape

On sunny weekend days, the Genoese escape the busy lanes of the city centre and head for the hills for walks, picnics and long, leisurely meals at rustic country restaurants. The **Funicolare Zecca-Righi** (Map p40, D2; Largo della Zecca) travels high above Genoa, stopping at several stations before reaching a terminus at Zecca-Righi. From there, you can make the 3km walk through woodlands of the Area Naturale della Mura and up to Forte Sperone, an abandoned fortification that was once an essential part of the city's 19th-century defences. From there, you can keep walking, all the way up past a series of other towers and forts, eventually leading to Forte Diamante. Perched on a ridge at 667m above sea level, this iconic 17th-century fortress offers sweeping 360-degree views over Genoa and the rolling, craggy hillsides surrounding the city.

Another option for a relaxing getaway is to take the narrow-gauge **Ferrovia Genova Casella** (Map p40; www.ferroviagenova casella.it; one way €4.50, family round-trip €20), which snakes 25km north from the cute Stazione di Genova Piazza Manin to the village of Casella in the Valle Scrivia. Memorable walks intersect at various stations along the way, including at Trensacaso, where you can pick up the trail heading west to Forte Diamante.

---

standards, they are also very good, using top-quality produce and with lots of fresh, green flourishes. (☑010 856 85 93; www.pizzeriasavo. it; Via Al Ponte Calvi 16; pizzas €12-20; ☺noon-3pm & 6.30-11.30pm Mon-Sat, 6.30-11.30pm Sun)

Trattoria da Maria   TRATTORIA €

12 ✖ MAP P40, F3

Brace yourself for the lunchtime mayhem here. This is a totally authentic, if well touristed, workers' trattoria and there's much squeezing into tiny tables, shouted orders and a fast and furious succession of plates plonked on tables. A daily hand-scrawled menu is a roll call of elemental favourites that keep all comers full and happy, along with the jugs of ridiculously cheap wine. (☑010 58 10 80; Vico Testadoro 14r; meals €10-20; ☺11.45am-2.45pm Mon-Sat, 6.15-10pm Thu & Fri)

Drinking

Cantine Matteotti   WINE BAR

13 🚇 MAP P40, D5

The Puccini wafting up the laneway gives you some clue that this is a special little place. The owners here have a passion for good music and brilliant wine, and will pour you some amazing local drops and stave off your hunger with creatively topped crostini, pesto lasagna or generous cheese platters. (☎010 868 70 00; Archivolto Baliano 4-6r; ⏰6pm-1am Sun-Thu, to 2am Fri & Sat)

Les Rouges COCKTAIL BAR

14 ⏳ MAP P40, D4

One of Genoa's surfeit of crumbling *palazzi* is being put to excellent use in this atmospheric cocktail bar. Three bearded, vest-wearing, red-headed brothers – the 'rouges' of the name – man the floor and shake up some of the city's best cocktails, using top-shelf ingredients and herbal or floral flavours such as chamomile and kaffir lime. (☎329 3490644; 1st fl, Piazza Campetto 8a; ⏰6-11.45pm Sun-Thu, to 12.45am Fri & Sat)

Malkovich COCKTAIL BAR

15 ⏳ MAP P40, D3

Tucked under the bar Groove, Malkovich is one of Genoa's most atmospheric and secretive drinking dens. To get in, you'll have to provide the password (check the Facebook page for the question, which you'll have to answer!). Once inside, flickering candles, upbeat jazz and vintage furnishings scattered about the various rooms evoke Prohibition-era glam. There's even an artfully placed

Teatro Carlo Felice

bathtub. (www.facebook.com/malkovichgenova; Via ai Quattro Canti di San Francesco 32r; ⏰9pm-1am Sun-Thu, to 3am Fri & Sat)

Scurreria Beer & Bagel BEER HALL

16 ⏳ MAP P40, D4

A little bit of Brooklyn or Melbourne in the *caruggi*, this brewpub packs out with Genoa's black-clad young people. There are over a dozen taps of local and imported beers and a staggering by-the-bottle list. And, yes, it does bagels, stuffed in a way that only Italians can do, along with other belly-liners. (Via di Scurreria 22r; ⏰6pm-1am Mon-Fri, from noon Sat & Sun; 📶)

Entertainment

Teatro Carlo Felice THEATRE

17 ⭐ MAP P40, E4

Genoa's stunning four-stage opera house with a seasonal opera program that's worth booking ahead for. (📞010 538 13 14; www.carlofelice.it; Passo Eugenio Montale 4)

Giardini Luzzati ARTS CENTRE

18 ⭐ MAP P40, D6

A multi-function alternative space that hosts live music, street festivals, archaeological walks, debates, workshops and other performances. A full program can be found online, or just drop by for a weekend beer and see what's on. (📞010 898 47 85; www.giardiniluzzati.it; Piazzetta Rostagno)

Shopping

Paccottiglia CONCEPT STORE

19 🔒 MAP P40, D5

This concept store has a trove of thoughtfully curated garments and one-of-a-kind accessories. You'll find soft cotton shirts and espadrilles by Danish firm Ichi, form-fitting briefs by Spain's The Nude Label and dresses by ethical fashion brand SKFK. There's also eye-catching bath products, canvas bags, notebooks and curious wall

Palatial Shopping

Even if you're not in the market for designer homewares, it's worth trotting up the noble stairs at **Via Garibaldi 12** (Map p40, E3; 📞010 253 03 65; www.viagaribaldi12.com; ⏱10am-2pm & 3.30-7pm Tue-Sat) just to be reminded how splendid a city Genoa can be. There's an incredibly canny collection of contemporary furniture and objects, set amid elegant columns, arched windows and baroque painted ceilings.

art. (www.facebook.com/paccottiglia; Via di Canneto Il Lungo 67; ⏱11.15am-7.30pm Tue-Fri, from 10am Sat)

Temide DESIGN

20 🔒 MAP P40, E4

A showcase of Ligurian creativity, Temide sells works by local artists and artisans, including delicate ceramics, eye-catching jewellery, colourfully embroidered bags, hand-painted silk scarves, homewares made from recycled materials, and art-naïf sculptures and paintings. In short, you'll find plenty of original gift ideas. Temide also has a store in Savona. (www.temidestore.it; Vico del Fieno 40; ⏱3.30-7.30pm Mon, 10.30am-2pm & 3.30-7.30pm Tue-Sat)

Explore ◉
Portofino Peninsula to Levanto

This strip of coast between the blue waters of the Mediterranean and the mountainous Ligurian hinterland is home to some of Italy's most elite resorts, including favourite Portofino and the Santa Margherita Ligure, yet it also retains pockets of extreme natural beauty and profound authenticity.

The Short List

○ **Portofino (p50)** *Enjoying an alfresco aperitivo followed by a walk along this famed Riviera hideout.*

○ **Abbazia di San Fruttuoso (p52)** *Hiking the lush forest trails en route to this spectacularly sited medieval abbey.*

○ **Camogli (p55)** *Feasting on seafood against a backdrop of sea and pastel-coloured villas.*

○ **Sestri Levante (p60)** *Exploring the cobblestone lanes and shoreline that has long enchanted visitors, including Hans Christian Andersen.*

○ **La Funivia Rapallo-Montallegro (p59)** *Taking the cable car from Rapallo to a hilltop sanctuary, with jaw-dropping views over the coast.*

Getting There & Around

🚃 There's frequent rail service from Genoa to Camogli, Santa Margherita Ligure, Rapallo, Sestri Levante and Levanto.

⛴ Golfo Paradiso SNC operates boats from Genoa's Porto Antico to Camogli (one way/return €10/17) and Portofino (€15/24). There's also boat service operated by Servizio Marittimo del Tigullio (www.traghettiportofino.it) that connects Rapallo, Santa Margherita Ligure, Portofino and San Fruttuoso.

Portofino Peninsula to Levanto Map on p54

Top Sight 📷
Portofino

*Even the trees are handsome in Portofino, a
small but perfectly coiffured coastal village that
sits on its own peninsula, seemingly upping the
exclusivity factor by mere geography. Hotels here
are hushed and headily priced, but a drink by
Portofino's yacht-filled harbour or a stroll around
its designer shops can be easily enjoyed on a day
trip from Genoa.*

◉ MAP P54, B2

Tourist Office

Via Roma 35

🕑10am-6pm summer,
10am-3pm Thu-Sun winter

Castello Brown

A flight of stairs signposted 'Salita San Giorgio' leads from the harbour and past the Chiesa di San Giorgio to Portofino's unusual **castle** (pictured; www.castellobrown.com; Via alla Penisola 13a; €5; ⏱10am-7pm summer, to 5pm Sat & Sun winter), a 10-minute walk altogether (do confirm it's open with the tourist office before setting out, as the castle often closes for private events). The Genoese-built bulwark saw action against the Venetians, Savoyards, Sardinians and Austrians, and later fell to Napoleon.

Parco Naturale Regionale di Portofino

The Portofino peninsula's 60km of narrow **trails** (www.parks.it/parco.portofino) are a world away from the sinuous sports-car-lined road from Santa Margherita. Many of them are absolutely remote and all of them are free of charge. The tourist office has maps.

A good but tough day hike (there are super-exposed sections) is the 18km coastal route from Camogli to Santa Margherita Ligure via San Fruttuoso and Portofino. There are handy train connections at both ends.

★ Top Tips

o Various boat-taxi operators around the harbour host snorkelling and sightseeing trips (from €30).

o Golfo Paradiso (www.golfoparadiso. it) runs ferries to Portofino from Santa Margherita Ligure (€7), Rapallo (€9) and in summer Genoa (€15).

o Bus 82 (www.atp-spa.it) runs to Portofino from outside the tourist office in Santa Margherita Ligure.

✕ Take a Break

The harbourside location of **Ristorante Puny** (☎0185 26 90 37; Piazza Martiri dell'Olivetta; meals €40-50; ⏱noon-3pm & 7-11pm Fri-Wed) is ideal for indulging in beautifully prepared seafood.

Situated at the base of Portofino's lighthouse, **Al Faro di Portofino** (☎320 3087036; Via alla Penisola 18) has mesmerising views over the sea from its clifftop terrace.

Top Sight 📷
Abbazia di San Fruttuoso

The San Fruttuoso abbey feels like a world removed from other parts of the Riviera. The medieval complex overlooks a serene stretch of coastline and can only be reached on foot or by boat. Apart from visiting the old building and lounging on the small beach, the real draw to a visit is hiking the pretty coastal trail to get here.

🎯 MAP P54, A1

www.visitfai.it/sanfruttuoso

adult/reduced €7.50/4

🕑10am-5.45pm summer, to 3.45pm winter

The Abbey

The hamlet's sensitively restored Benedictine abbey was built as a final resting place for Bishop St Fructuosus of Tarragona, martyred in Spain in AD 259. It was rebuilt in the mid-13th century with the assistance of the Doria family. The abbey fell into decay with the decline of the religious community; by the 19th century it was divided into small living quarters. Today it has a calm simplicity and its charming everyday collection of ancient monkish things feels touchingly close and human.

Christ of the Abyss

In 1954 a bronze statue of Christ was lowered 17m to the seabed, offshore from the abbey, to bless the waters. The open-armed savior was sculpted by the artist Guido Galletti, and placed near the site where Italian diver Dario Gonzatti died in 1947. You can either dive to see it or, if the waters are calm, take a boat tour run by the Golfo Paradiso SNC.

Hiking Trails

There are numerous walking paths to the abbey, though the most popular access points are from Camogli or Portofino; allow about 2½ hours from either town. Wherever you start, be prepared for some steep climbing as you cross the hilly peninsula. Coming from Camogli, there are two ways to reach the abbey: on an inland path via Semaforo Nuovo (marked by two ride triangles) or a coastal path via the Batterie (marked by two red circles). The latter has some short but treacherous stretches across open cliff faces, with chains lending extra support – not recommended for those afraid of heights.

★ Top Tips

o If you're not hiking, you can come by boat from Camogli (one way/return €9/14), Portofino (€9/13), Santa Margherita Ligure (€11/17) and, in summer, Genoa (€15/24).

o San Fruttuoso gets incredibly crowded in the warmer months. If hiking, go very early in the morning to beat the crowds.

o Dining options are limited. To avoid disappointment, come prepared with your own picnic.

✕ Take a Break

Da Laura (☎339 5208537; meals €36-46; ◷12.30-2pm) serves outstanding seafood dishes, with outdoor dining on a shaded terrace. Reserve ahead.

There's also a snack bar where you can pick up focaccia, cold drinks and other snacks just above the beach.

Portofino Peninsula to Levanto

San Pietro
Vara

Carro

Mattarana

A12

Bonassola

Levanto ⊙5

Parco Nazionale delle
Cinque Terre

Punta Meso

Framura

Deiva
Marina

Moneglia

Casarza
Ligure

Carasco

Zoagli

Rapallo

uGianeu

Santa
Margherita
Ligure

Parco Naturale Regionale
di Portofino

⊙ Portofino

Chiavari

Lavagna

Cavi

A12

Sestri ⊙4
Levante

Recco

Camogli ⊙1

La Cucina di
Nonna Nina

Centro Visito
Batterie Silvio
Sommazzi

⊙ Abbazia
di San
Fruttuoso

Ligurian Sea

For reviews see	
⊙ Top Sights	p50
⊙ Sights	p55

10 km

5 miles

A B C D E F

1 2 3 4

Camogli

1 ⊙ MAP P54, A1

Camogli, 25km east of Genoa, is most famous for its sheer number of *trompe l'œil* villas, its photogenic terraced streets winding down to a perfect cove of pebble beach amid a backdrop of umbrella pines and olive groves. While tourists flock to Portofino, this is where many of northern Italy's intellectuals and creatives have their summer apartments. Still, as pretty as the town is, it remains a working fishing hub – the town's name means 'house of wives', hailing from the days when the womenfolk ran the show while the husbands were away at sea.

Centro Visito Batterie Silvio Sommazzi   HISTORIC SITE

This free visitor centre provides insight into the military installations scattered in the surrounding hillside. The 202nd Batteria Chiappa guarded the coast during the WWII, and you can still poke around the various bunkers, sentinel posts, barracks and armoury (pick up a map to see the layout). The visitor centre runs one-hour guided tours of the military post. (☑348 0182556; www.parcoportofino. com; Chiappa; guided tour adult/child €5/3; ⏱10am-5pm Sat & Sun Mar–mid-Jun & Sep)

Mercato   MARKET

Camogli's Wednesday market is a big draw, with vendors spreading their wares on Via XX Settembre,

Camogli

Via Schiaffino e Piazza Schiaffino. (Via XX Settembre; ⊙8am-1pm)

La Cucina di Nonna Nina TRATTORIA €€

In the leafy heights of San Rocco di Camogli you'll find the only Slow Food–recommended restaurant along the coast, named for grand-mother Nina, whose heirloom recipes have been adapted with love by Paolo Delphin. Your culinary odyssey will include fabulous traditional dishes such as air-dried cod stewed with pine nuts, potatoes and local Taggiasca olives, and *rossetti* (minnow) and artichoke soup. (📞0185 77 38 35; www.nonnanina.it; Via F Molfino 126; meals €35-50; ⊙12.30-3pm & 7.30-10.30pm Thu-Tue)

Da Paolo SEAFOOD €€

Up a back lane from the water-front, stylish Da Paolo has the town's best fish and seafood, all fresh off the boats and done in a variety of simple local styles. Order fish by the *etto* (100g) or plates of scampi or squid. Pastas include a fabulous fish ravioli. (📞0185 77 35 95; www.ristorantedapaolocamogli. com; Via San Fortunato 14; meals €40-50; ⊙noon-2.30pm & 7.30-10.30pm Wed-Sun, 7.30-10.30pm Tue)

Revello BAKERY €

If you're not on a mission to taste-test every town's *focacceria*, Revello is a suitably respectable choice if you had to choose just one. Pick up slices of its *focaccia di Recco* – a slightly flaky variety stuffed with stracchino cheese –

Villa Durazzo

or others topped with anchovies, fresh tomatoes and Ligurian olives, or go for the plainer sage or onion topped loaves. (☑0185 77 07 77; www.revellocamogli.com; Via Garibaldi 183; focaccia from €2; ⏰8am-7.30pm)

La Bossa di Mario   SEAFOOD €€

You'll drink your fill of over 130 fine local and Italian wines in this elegant bar. To accompany them, choose something off the seasonal menu, such as Camogli tuna on a bed of the sweetest vine tomatoes, the raw fish of the day with a squeeze of citrus and fragrant coriander, or cannelloni stuffed with the local favourite green (borage) and scallops. (☑0185 77 25 05; www.labossa.it; Via della Repubblica 124; meals €28-38; ⏰6pm-midnight Thu-Tue)

La Mancina   BAR

A couple of stools outside will give you a sea view, but the real action here is inside, where books line the walls and locals chat with the welcoming owner over *spritzes* or local wines. (Via al Porto Camogli; ⏰5pm-2am Thu-Tue)

Santa Margherita Ligure

2 ◉ MAP P54, B1

Santa Margherita Ligure materialises like a calm impressionist painting. You wouldn't want to change a single detail of the picture-perfect seaside promenade in this fishing village

Punta Chiappa

From Camogli's main esplanade, Via Garibaldi, boats sail to the Punta Chiappa (one way/return €6/11), a rocky outcrop on the Portofino promontory where you can swim and sunbathe like an Italian. By sea it's a 5-minute trip; otherwise it's a picturesque 3km walk along the trail that begins at the end of Via San Bartolomeo.

turned retirement spot, where elegant hotels with Liberty facades overlook yachts. It's decidedly less bling than Portofino, with some affordable hotel options and a surprisingly workaday town behind the waterfront.

Villa Durazzo   GARDENS

This exquisitely turned-out mansion and gardens, part of a 16th-century castle complex, overlooks the sea. In the lavish Italian gardens, you can take an aromatic stroll among lemon trees, hydrangea and camellia hedges, and other flora typical of the town's mild climate, or wander among its recently restored collection of 17th-century paintings.

A cafe is open year-round and the terrace makes a lovely setting for a drink. (www.villadurazzo.it; Piazzale San Giacomo 3; gardens free, villa adult/child €5.50/3; ⏰gardens 9am-7pm, villa 9am-1pm & 2-6pm)

Santuario di Nostra Signora della Rosa CHURCH

You'll gasp audibly when entering Santa Margherita Ligure's small yet lavish baroque church, not just at the truly dazzling array of gold leaf, frescoes, chandeliers and stained glass, but also at the sheer serendipity of it being here at all. (Piazza Caprera)

L'Altro Eden SEAFOOD €€

A seafood place right on the docks, yes, but this grey-and-white streamlined vaulted space is a maritime kitsch-free zone. It's romantic and cosy on colder evenings; outside tables are right by the boats in summer. Fish is done by weight and to order, but is best known for *crudo* (raw fish) and risotto with fresh prawns or, in season, squid ink. (📞0185 29 30 56; www.laltro.ristoranteeden.com; Calata del Porto 11; meals €40-60; 🕐noon-11.30pm Mon-Fri, noon-2.30pm & 7-11.30pm Sat & Sun)

Sabot Italia BAR

Just around the corner from the historic centre, Sabot serves some of Santa Margherita Ligure's best *aperitivi*, where a generous platter of snacks accompanies the drink orders from 5pm to 9pm. Sink into one of the sofas, or grab a streetside table and enjoy the well-made cocktails, upbeat jazzy grooves, and friendly banter with the staff. (www.facebook.com/sabotitalia; Piazza Martiri della Libertà 32; 🕐5pm-3am Mon-Fri, from 10am Sat & Sun; 📶)

Rapallo

3 ⊙ MAP P54, B1

WB Yeats, Max Beerbohm and Ezra Pound all garnered inspiration in Rapallo and it's not difficult to see why. With its bright-blue changing cabins, palm-fringed beach and diminutive 16th-century castle perched above the sea, the town has a poetic and nostalgic air. It's at its busiest on Thursdays, when market stalls spread along the waterfront.

Lungomare Vittorio Veneto AREA

Rapallo's scenic seafront promenade hosts a daily parade of locals and visitors. This is also the setting for the Mercato del Giovedì (Thursday market).

uGiancu LIGURIAN €€

About 5km inland in the hamlet of San Massimo di Rapallo, this cult restaurant is run by comic-book collector Fausto Oneto, and half of his collection decorates the walls. Away from the coast, the cooking focuses on meat and vegetables, including an incredibly succulent herb-battered suckling lamb with field greens from the kitchen gardens. (📞0185 26 05 05; www.ugiancu.it; Via San Massimo 78; meals €30-40; 🕐8-10.30pm Thu-Tue, noon-3pm Sun Dec-Oct)

Vecchia Rapallo SEAFOOD €€

Seafood is the star here, and it's done well with the occasional creative touch. House-made stuffed pastas have particular appeal – the sea bream ravioli comes with beetroot and prawn sauce, while a chard-filled variety comes with truffle sauce. There's a cocktail and wine bar if you're just after a drink, too. (☎0185 5 00 53; www.vecchiarapallo.com; Via Cairoli 20/24; meals €28-48; ☺noon-2.30pm & 6-11pm summer, reduced hours winter)

Ö Bansin
TRATTORIA €

Ligurian comfort food – salt cod fritters, chickpea soup, spinach-stuffed pasta with walnut sauce, mussels gratin – gets served up here with a minimum of fuss and not just a little bit of love. Lunch menus, with two courses and house wine or water, are €10

Hilltop Sanctuary

When you've had your fill of Rapallo's promenade poseurs, rise above them in a 1934-vintage funicular – aka **La Funivia Rapallo-Montallegro** (Piazzale Solari 2; one way/return €5.50/8; ☺9am-12.30pm & 2-6pm). You'll soon be whisked up to the Santuario Basilica di Montallegro (612m), built on the spot where, in 1557, the Virgin Mary was reportedly sighted. Those who prefer to go on foot from Rapallo can follow an old mule track (5km, 1½ hours) to the hilltop site.

Other walking paths intersect at the top, including a scenic trail down to Chiavari.

La Funivia Rapallo-Montallegro

(or €5 with just a first course and side), and there's a garden courtyard to enjoy in summer. (📞0185 23 11 19; www.trattoriabansin.it; Via Venezia 105; meals €18-27; 🕑noon-2pm Mon, noon-2pm & 7-9.30pm Tue-Sun)

Parla Come Mangi
FOOD & DRINKS

A short stroll from the waterfront, this delightfully enticing deli is packed to the ceiling with delicacies from the Italian Riviera and beyond. You'll find cheeses, salumi, wines, olive oils, handmade pastas, jams and sweets. There's no better place to assemble a picnic. (www.parlacomemangi.com; Via Mazzini 44; 🕑8am-1pm & 4-8pm Mon-Sat)

Sestri Levante

4 ◎ MAP P54, D2

Located roughly halfway between Genoa and Cinque Terre, the pretty seaside town of Sestri Levante has enchanted countless generations of visitors. Hans Christian Andersen fell for the setting while renting a room here in 1833. **Baia delle Favole** (Bay of Fables), the long palm-fringed shoreline, was later named in his honour. Beachfront aside, Sestri Levante also has a small historic quarter, sprinkled with Liberty-style buildings, easygoing shops, cafes and alfresco restaurants.

Just south of the cobblestones is the scenic **Baia del Silenzio** (Bay of Silence), with a small

Baia del Silenzio

pretty beach backed by scenic villas. There are also some fine walks leading south of town, which offer dramatic views overlooking a town sometimes described as having 'due mari' (two seas).

Museo Archeologico e della Città   MUSEUM

Spread across the 3rd and 4th floors of the photogenic Palazzo Fascie, Musel delves into Sestri Levante's past with interactive exhibitions and displays of archaeological finds – some of which were uncovered from underwater sites. The scope is quite broad and features works from the Palaeolithic period, the Roman era and the Middle Ages. The 3rd floor takes you up into the 20th century, addressing major upheavals in the region, war and the rise of industry. (Musel; www.musel.it; Corso Colombo 50; adult/child €5/3; ⏰10am-1pm & 2-5pm)

Chiesa di Santa Maria Immacolata   CHURCH

It's a short but steep climb up to this 17th-century church, which is known for its finely crafted wooden altarpiece. You'll also find here a delightful presepe (nativity scene), just to the left after entering the church. Press the button to bring the scene to life – complete with thunder and lightning, masticating cows, flickering fires, and dozens of mechanised villagers (cobblers,

fishers, knife sharpeners and even card players).

The small plaza in front offers a fabulous view over the Baia del Silenzio. (Chiesa dei Cappuccini; Via Cappuccini)

Osteria Mattana   LIGURIAN €

A cellar-like two-room restaurant beloved by locals, Osteria Mattana serves up hearty home-cooked dishes at outstanding prices. The chalkboard menu changes daily and might include cuttlefish stew with potatoes and artichokes, spaghetti with mussels and clams, or braised rabbit. Start off with farinata (chickpea-flour flatbread) fired up from the wood-burning oven in front. Cash only. (☎0185 45 76 33; www.osteriamattana.com; Via XXV Aprile 34; meals €20-30; ⏰7-10.30pm daily May-Sep, closed Mon & also open noon-2.30pm Sat & Sun Oct-Apr)

Black Bart   BAR

In a cosy drinking den located near the Baia del Silenzio, Black Bart serves up the city's best cocktails. Try a creative elixir like Le Vigne Sospese, featuring cinar (an Italian bitter) mezcal, angostura and chocolate bitter. Outstanding wines, friendly service and satisfying cheese and charcuterie platters add to the appeal. (www.facebook.com/black bartwine; Via Cappuccini 7; ⏰5pm-1.30am Wed-Mon)

Levanto

5  MAP P54, F4

Just north of Monterosso, the slumbering seaside town of Levanto (*lay*-vahn-toh) makes a fine base for exploring Cinque Terre with somewhat smaller crowds. A settlement has existed here since the Roman times (when it was known as Ceula), with fragments of its storied past still sprinkled around town. Among other things, Levanto is home to a UNESCO-listed 13th-century *loggia*, a rare example of late medieval architecture that survives intact.

Most visitors, however, come for the wide pebble-and-sand beach, with a scenic promenade elevated above the shoreline. Levanto is the starting point for a gorgeous walk (p64) to Monterosso over the Punta Mesco. You can also hire a bike for a spin to the nearby villages of Bonassola and Framura beyond.

Via Guani   STREET

This atmospheric lane, located a few blocks from the beach, winds its way past some of Levanto's oldest buildings. Don't miss stately former noble residences like No 37, known as Palazzo delle Sirene, dating back to the 16th century. The street intersects with the picturesque Piazza del Popolo, where you'll find the *loggia medievale,* its columns hiding a small enclosure with the remains of a 13th-century fresco.

Biking along Bonassola's beach

Biking to Bonassola

From Levanto, you can hire a bike for a short but pleasant ride to several other villages along a smooth, flat promenade. The tranquil settlement of Bonassola lies just 2.5km north of Levanto, and it has flower-lined streets, a few seafood restaurants and a stretch of grey sand beach framed by forested hills. The ride here follows an abandoned railway line that's been converted into a biking and pedestrian thoroughfare, which encompasses a series of well-lit train tunnels that open up every few hundred metres to striking views of wave-dashed cliffs and rocky shoreline.

Once in Bonassola, you can stop for refreshment at one of the outdoor cafes just one block back from the waterfront or time your visit to coincide with a meal at **Osteria Antica Guetta** (📞0187 81 37 97; Via Marconi 1; meals €30-40; ⏰noon-3pm & 7-11pm Thu-Tue) overlooking the shoreline. Afterwards, you can continue another 3km to the village of Framura. This stretch is mostly through dark, dripping tunnels so it's a rather dreary walk, but an intriguing (and fast) bike ride. Several outfitters in Levanto rent out bikes, including **Sensafreni Bike Shop** (📞0187 80 71 28; Piazza del Popolo 1; bike hire per hour/half day/full day from €3/5/15; ⏰9am-1pm & 4-8pm Mon-Sat), located a short stroll from the waterfront.

Ristorante Moresco
LIGURIAN €€

Situated in a vaulted-ceiling dining room a few blocks from the beach, Ristorante Moresco is a chef-driven restaurant that has a loyal local following for its superb seafood and pasta dishes served at reasonable prices. Stuffed mussels, *spaghetti alle vongole* (spaghetti with clams), sea bass ravioli and *pansotti alla genovese* (stuffed pasta with walnut sauce) are among the many standout dishes. Be sure to reserve ahead. (📞0187 80 72 53; Via Jacopo da Levanto 24; meals €30-40; ⏰noon-2pm & 7-10pm)

Contro Vento
BAR

A short hop from the beach (via a tunnel), Contro Vento is a friendly spot for refreshment from morning to night. There's Franziskaner and Leffe on draught, good wines by the glass, and first-rate cocktails – plus focaccia sandwiches, *caprese* or anchovy salads, and cheese platters. Grab a seat at one of the umbrella-shaded tables out front, and let the day unfold. (Corso Italia 17; ⏰8am-10pm; 📶)

Walking Tour 🚶

Levanto to Monterosso

This walk takes in Mediterranean forest, sea cliffs and breathtaking overlooks. It also offers a window into the past, with stops at a 13th-century castle and the ruins of a medieval monastery. The highlight is the view from atop Punta Mesco, where you'll be able to see all five Cinque Terre villages tucked along this jagged stretch of coast.

Walk Facts

Start Levanto beach; train Levanto

End Monterosso; train Monterosso

Length 7km; three hours

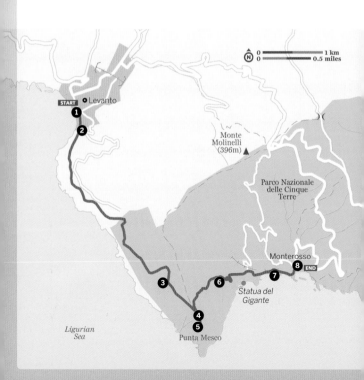

❶ Seaside of Levanto

Begin the walk on the shoreline of **Levanto**. Walk towards the southern end of the promenade and admire the view from this underrated coastal town. Take the marked stairway just past the stone columns on your left.

❷ Castello di Levanto

These stairs go up through an old part of the village and past Levanto's beautifully preserved 13th-century **castle**. This photogenic fortification, complete with crenellated towers, fulfilled many roles over the years – including as a prison in the 18th century. Today it is privately owned.

❸ Podere Case Lovara

FAI (the National Trust for Italy) is restoring an abandoned **agricultural site** overlooking the Ligurian Sea. Olive groves, new drystone walls, fruit trees and vegetable gardens, and rebuilt farm dwellings are transforming this ruin into a place of beauty and productivity. If volunteers are around, you're welcome to take a look at the work that they're doing or have a picnic on the property (small donations requested).

❹ Punta Mesco

The path ascends along rocky soil, through pines, holm oaks and Mediterranean scrub, with the views becoming more majestic over the cliff faces at each curve in the trail. You'll soon be at a prime panoramic spot on the **Punta Mesco**. Atop this lofty promontory you'll be able to see both the bay of Levanto and the bay of Monterosso.

❺ Eremo di Sant'Antonio

The ruins of this **hermitage** dedicated to St Anthony lie at the end of a short (300m) spur off the main trail. The site dates back to the 1300s, and was gradually abandoned over the centuries. The brothers here kept an eye out for pirate ships on the horizon and lit signal fires to warn nearby villages of approaching corsairs.

❻ Monterosso Views

You'll have fabulous **views** as you begin the descent towards Monterosso. After many stairs, the edge of the beach comes into view, with Fegina, Monterosso's modern half just beyond.

❼ Spiaggia di Fegina

Fegina's pretty **beach** makes a fine spot to relax after a long walk. You'll find free stretches sandwiched between the pay areas. And this is the only proper beach in Cinque Terre.

❽ Monterosso

End your walk in the historic centre of **Monterosso** (p67), reached by taking the car-pedestrian tunnel located a few hundred metres past the train station. Here you'll find plenty of options to refuel, with alfresco restaurants sprinkled on and near Via Roma.

Explore ⊚
Monterosso

The most accessible village by car and the only Cinque Terre settlement to sport a proper stretch of beach, the westernmost Monterosso is the least quintessential of the quintet. The village, known for its lemon trees and anchovies, is delightful. Split in two, its new and old halves are linked by an underground tunnel burrowed beneath the blustery San Cristoforo promontory.

The Short List

○ **Convento dei Cappuccini (p68)** Peering back through the centuries at this medieval convent overlooking the coast.

○ **Santuario della Madonna di Soviore (p74)** Making the steep ascent to this lofty forest-fringed sanctuary high above the village.

○ **Il Massimo della Focaccia (p73)** Grabbing a slice of fabulous, fresh-baked focaccia and enjoying it down on Monterosso's rocky beach.

○ **Enoteca Internazionale (p76)** Tasting your way through the wines of Cinque Terre at this terrace cafe and wine shop.

○ **Fabbrica d'Arte Monterosso (p76)** Browsing for locally made ceramics and other gift ideas on the village lanes.

Getting There & Around

🚃 Monterosso is on the main train line for the Trenitalia Cinque Terre Express trains.

🚗 Monterosso has the largest parking area of all the villages.

Monterosso Map on p72

Monterosso beach NICOLE CONSOLI / EYEEM / GETTY IMAGES ©

Top Sight 📷
Convento dei Cappuccini

On a promontory perched above the village of Monterosso, the Convent of Capuchin Friars has been around for over 400 years, and remains a much-loved part of village life. The short but steep climb up offers magical views and the chance to peer inside the jewel box of a church with some surprising works of art, including a lush painting by Van Dyck.

◉ **MAP P72, B5**

Salita San Cristoforo

Chiesa di San Francesco

From a distance, the facade seems to be made of marble. But in fact, it's a fine *trompe l'œil*: just stucco painted in black and white stripes. Inside, one of the great treasures of the monastery hangs on the left side of the church. Christ on the cross, flanked by two exquisitely painted figures, is a masterpiece attributed to Flemish painter Van Dyck, who spent many years in the Italian Riviera. It's worth paying the €1, which will illuminate fine details in the painting. Note the skull at the base of the cross, the lifelike quality of the figures and the eclipse of the sun on the right side of the painting.

Cemetery

Keep walking uphill from the church, and you'll soon reach the village cemetery. This was once where an 11th-century castle stood, surrounded by stout walls to protect against pirate attacks. Today, the ground amid the crumbling old walls serves as the final resting place for villagers and parish priests. Some fine monuments stretch toward the sky, and if you wind your way up through the cemetery, you'll reach another fine lookout.

St Francis & the Wolf

On the walk up to the convent, a bronze sculpture of St Francis and his lupine friend (pictured) sits on a gorgeous lookout over the seaside. With outstretched arm and paw, the pair indicate a stretch of mountain-backed coastline, with each of the tiny Cinque Terre villages visible from here.

★ **Top Tips**

◦ Be respectful when visiting the church, and even more so when venturing into the cemetery. Locals still pay their respects at family tombs. Don't eat or drink here: picnicking is strictly *vietato* (forbidden)!

◦ You can reach the convent from the old Monterosso centre. You can also get there coming directly from the train station – just take the seaside path, rather than entering the tunnel.

✕ **Take a Break**

If coming directly from the new part of town, stop first at Il Massimo della Focaccia (p73), which serves delicious focaccia slices and other snacks.

In the old town, San Martino Gastronomia (p73) has a small menu of changing – but always exceptional – daily specials.

Monterosso Convento dei Cappuccini

Walking Tour 🚶

Monterosso

Strolling Cinque Terre's westernmost village, you'll have some fine views over the beachfront, and get a look at the new part of town, before crossing into the old lanes of its tiny historic centre. World War II ruins, a medieval church and hilltop panoramas are also part of the Monterosso experience.

Walk Facts

Start Statua del Gigante;
🚌 Monterosso

End Via Roma;
🚌 Monterosso

Length 2.2km; two hours

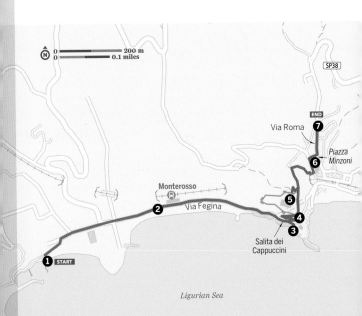

❶ Statua del Gigante

Start your walk at the western (newer) end of Monterosso. On a small cliff fringing the beach stand the remains of a 14m-high giant Neptune, **Statua del Gigante**, built in 1910 to hold up the seaward edge of the Villa Palatine. The god of the sea has suffered damages over the years, though it was once a much-photographed symbol of Monterosso.

❷ Promenade

Walking eastward, you'll soon reach the **promenade** above the sea. Here you'll have a fine view over the pebbly beach, which fills up with sunbathers during the summer. Terrace cafes make fine spots to take in the scene, and you can also grab a gelato, an espresso or a slice of focaccia as you continue east.

❸ Pillbox

Instead of entering the tunnel through the hillside, take the path leading up to the right. You'll soon reach stairs leading down to a restaurant, and just beyond an old **pillbox** built by the Germans to repel an Allied invasion during WWII. Watch your step if you decide to go down for a closer look.

❹ Monumento di San Francesco d'Assisi

Take the stairs that lead further up the cliff and turn right to reach the **Monumento di San Francesco d'Assisi**. The statue of the holy man and his friend the wolf enjoy a fabulous view over the seaside. On clear days you can see all five Cinque Terre villages.

❺ Convento dei Cappuccini

Keep heading uphill to eventually reach the **Convento dei Cappuccini** (p68). The black-and-white-striped church dates from the 17th century, and houses a painting of the crucifixion attributed to Van Dyck. Other fine works in the church include *Christ Scorned* by Bernardo Castello and *La Veronica* by Bernardo Strozzi.

❻ Chiesa San Giovanni Battista

Descend into the village and stop by an even older architectural treasure, the striped **Chiesa San Giovanni Battista** (p73). This Gothic church dates from the early 14th century and has a few notable works within, including a painting of the Madonna del Rosario, attributed to the school of Luca Cambiaso.

❼ Via Roma

End your wander in the heart of old Monterosso on the lively **Via Roma**. This street is lined with shops, restaurants and wine bars. Treat yourself to a glass of Cinque Terre's finest at the Enoteca Internazionale (p76). The terrace is well placed for watching village life unfold.

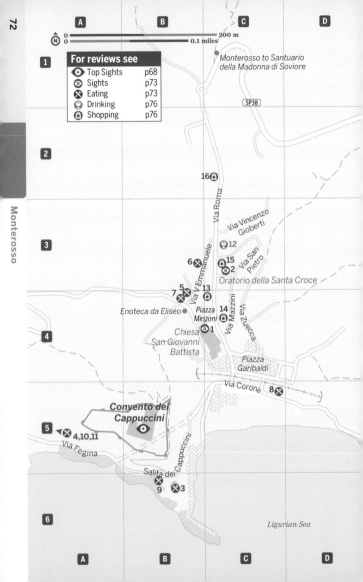

For reviews see

◉ Top Sights	p68
◉ Sights	p73
✖ Eating	p73
🍷 Drinking	p76
🛍 Shopping	p76

Monterosso to Santuario
della Madonna di Soviore

SP38

Via Roma

Via Vincenzo
Gioberti

16🛍

🍷12

Via San
Pietro

6✖ 🛍15

Oratorio della Santa Croce

5✖
7✖ 13

Via V Emmanuele

Enoteca da Eliseo ●

Piazza
Minzoni

14 🛍

Via Mazzini

◉2

◉1

Via Zuecca

Chiesa
San Giovanni
Battista

Piazza
Garibaldi

Via Corone   8✖

**Convento dei
Cappuccini**

◉

✖4,10,11
5
Via Fegina

Salita dei
Cappuccini

9✖   ✖3

Ligurian Sea

200 m
0.1 miles

Sights

Chiesa San Giovanni Battista
CHURCH

1 ⊙ MAP P72, C4

One of the oldest churches in Cinque Terre, San Giovanni Battista has a striped facade dating back to 1307. The Ligurian-Gothic design features white and dark-green marble and a large rose window with lace-like ornamentation. Note the fresco of John the Baptist over the entrance.

Two plaques located on the side of the building show the high-water marks that were left during the floods in 1966 and 2011. There are also photos located inside the church that reveal the damages wrought in October 2011. (Via Roma 12)

Oratorio della Santa Croce
CHRISTIAN SITE

2 ⊙ MAP P72, C3

This was the seat for one of two confraternities (secular associations that were dedicated to doing charitable works) in Monterosso which was active from the 15th to the 17th centuries. The Santa Croce group wore white robes, tended the sick and the poor, and ran a village hospital. The small church has baroque elements, with a lavish mural above the altar. Near the organ at the back, a small model of a sailing ship seems to float in mid-air. (Via San Pietro 8)

Eating

Torre Aurora
LIGURIAN €€€

3 🍴 MAP P72, B6

Monterosso's most memorable setting for a meal is undoubtedly this 13th-century tower with a terrace overlooking the sea. Painstakingly prepared seafood (squid-ink pasta with anchovies), mouth-watering grass-fed Fassona beef and excellent wines go nicely with the sweeping views. You can also stop by for an afternoon *aperitivo*, or a postdinner nightcap (during summer the bar stays open until midnight). (☑ 366 1453702; www.torreauroracinqueterre.com; Via Bastione 5; meals €50-60; ⊙ noon-10.30pm Apr-Oct)

Il Massimo della Focaccia
STREET FOOD €

4 🍴 MAP P72, A5

Just below the train station, this photogenic takeaway fires up the best focaccia in all of Cinque Terre. You can order that perfectly crisped bread topped with pesto, tomatoes and olives, sweet onions, with cheese or in various other fashions. There's also quiche-like *torta* (savoury pie) and a few sweet dessert items. (Via Fegina 50; focaccia €2-5; ⊙ 9am-6pm Thu-Tue)

San Martino Gastronomia
LIGURIAN €

5 🍴 MAP P72, B3

The go-to place for delicious market-fresh fair at reasonable

Santuario della Madonna di Soviore

From Via Roma in the village, follow trail 509 up through forest and past the ruins of an old hexagonal chapel to an **ancient paved mule path** (Map p72, C1) that leads to Soviore, the Italian Riviera's oldest sanctuary, dating from the 11th century. Here you'll find a bar, a restaurant and views as far as Corsica on a clear day. It's a two-hour walk to get there.

Reach the trailhead by taking Via Roma up through town; just after the roundabout, take the stairs (signed with trail markers) off to the left.

prices, San Martino has a changing chalkboard menu posted out front and just a couple of tables for the lucky few; most locals order to take away. Linguine with seafood, grilled swordfish and *pansotti* (a stuffed pasta) with walnuts are among the many hits. (☑346 1860764; Via San Martino 3; mains €9-13; ⏰noon-3pm & 6-8.30pm Tue-Sun)

Trattoria da Oscar   SEAFOOD €€
6 ✖ MAP P72, B3

Behind Piazza Matteoti, in the heart of the old town, this tiny vaulted dining room is run by a young, friendly team and attracts a loyal local crowd. The town's famed anchovies dominate the small menu;

there's also excellent gnocchi with pesto, seafood spaghetti and grilled swordfish. There are some lovely laneway tables. Reserve ahead. Cash only. (☑345 8714789; Via V Emanuele 67; meals €32-42; ⏰noon-2.30pm & 7-9.30pm Fri-Wed)

Da Eraldo   LIGURIAN €
7 ✖ MAP P72, B4

One of the liveliest restaurants in town, Eraldo's is a family-style spot where you dine amid arched brick ceilings and red-and-white table-cloths, with the songs of Andrea Bocelli wafting overhead. Sure, it's a bit of a cliché, but the unfussy home-style cooking is quite good (Eraldo honed his cooking skills from the village grandmothers), and the prices and portion sizes are excellent. (☑366 3388440; Piazza Giacomo Matteotti 6; meals €22-34; ⏰noon-2.30pm & 6.30-9.30pm Fri-Wed)

Ristorante Belvedere   SEAFOOD €€
8 ✖ MAP P72, C5

With tables overlooking the beach, this unpretentious seafood restaurant is a good place to try the local bounty. Start with *penne con scampi* (pasta tubes with scampi) before diving into *zuppa di pesce* (fish soup). Or partake of the speciality, the amphora Belvedere (€49 for two), where lobsters, mussels, clams, octopus and swordfish are stewed in a herb-scented broth in traditional

earthenware. (📞0187 81 70 33; www.
ristorante-belvedere.it; Piazza Garibaldi
38; meals €30-40; 🕐noon-2.30pm &
7-9.30pm Wed-Mon)

L'Ancora della Tortuga

LIGURIAN €€

9 🍴 MAP P72, B6

Perched on a cliff overlooking
the crashing waves, this long-
running spot serves high-end
seafood-topped pastas, grilled fish
and roast meat dishes in a cosy
rock-walled dining room decorated with nautical knick-knacks.
You can also dine alfresco on the
terrace above. (📞0187 80 00 65;
www.ristorantetortuga.it; Salita dei
Cappuccini 4; meals €40-60, menu
€40; 🕐12.30-3.30pm & 6.30-9.30pm
Tue-Sun Mar-Oct)

Miky

SEAFOOD €€€

10 🍴 MAP P72, A5

If you're looking for something a
little more elegant than a seafront
fry-up, Miky does a seasonal fish
menu in a moody, modern dining
room. Booking ahead is advised.
If you miss out on a table, casual
beach-side tables are available
at its *cantina* (wine bar); ask for
directions. (📞0187 81 76 08; www.
ristorantemiky.it; Via Fegina 104; meals
€55-80; 🕐noon-2.30pm & 7-10pm
Wed-Mon Apr-Oct)

Slurp!

GELATO €

11 🍴 MAP P72, A5

Across from the seaside promenade, Slurp! is an obligatory stop
when strolling the waterfront.
House-made gelato comes in a

Chiesa San Giovanni Battista (p73)

Enoteca da Eliseo

Going strong since the 1980s, this back-lane **wine bar** (Map p72, B4; ☑ 0187 81 73 08; www.enotecadaeliseo.com; Piazza Giacomo Matteotti 3; ⏰ 2-11pm Wed-Mon) run by the welcoming Eliseo and Mary makes a charming setting for a glass or two. Grab an outdoor table and enjoy an outstanding selection of wines, grappas and other libations. The lemon spritz (featuring a locally made *limoncino*) is quite refreshing on warm days.

variety of rich flavours including local favourite *crema al limone di Monterosso* (lemon cream). (Via Fegina 86; gelato €2.20-3.20)

Drinking

Enoteca Internazionale   WINE BAR

12 🚻 MAP P72, C3

One of the best places in Cinque Terre to discover the wines of the region, this family-run wine shop offers various tastings from its selection of over 500 different wines. On clear days, you can enjoy those flights (€15 to €25) and wines by the glass (€4.50 to €6) from the small terrace in front. You can also pair wines with food. (☑ 0187 81 72 78; www.enotecainternazionale.com; Via Roma 62; ⏰ noon-midnight Apr-Oct)

Shopping

Fabbrica d'Arte Monterosso   ARTS & CRAFTS

13 🔒 MAP P72, C3

Several generations of one family create and sell the beautiful ceramics on display at this shop on Via Roma. Vases, bowls, jugs, platters and decorative tiles feature elegant designs – the narrow anchovy-shaped serving platter makes a fine conversation piece and memento. You'll also find a small selection of jewellery and 100% hand-printed linen products (tea towels, beach towels, tablecloths, runners).

There's a smaller second branch of the shop located around the corner at Via V Emanuele 27. (☑ 0187 81 74 88; www.fabbricadarte.com; Via Roma 9; ⏰ 10am-7pm Mar-Oct, to 10pm Jun-Aug)

Enoteca Ciak   FOOD & DRINKS

14 🔒 MAP P72, C4

Located near the entrance to the old part of town, Ciak is a good first stop for picking up gourmet food items: high-quality olive oils, pastas and *limoncino* (lemon liqueur), plus one of Monterosso's best selections of wine. There are a few non-edible souvenirs here, including pottery. Many products are locally (or regionally) sourced. (Via Roma 4; ⏰ 9am-9pm)

Enoteca Ciak

Lanapo
FASHION & ACCESSORIES

15 MAP P72, C3

This boutique seems like it was plucked straight from Milan and plunked onto the cobblestones of Monterosso – perhaps not surprising given designer Federica Napoletano's Milanese roots. Her artfully handcrafted Lanapo sandals have, in fact, been featured in numerous fashion mags, and are versatile enough for both urban high style and more relaxed days on the shore. (347 3071570; www.lanapo.it; Via Roma 48; 11am-6.30pm mid-Apr–Oct, to 9pm Jun-Aug)

Five Lands
FOOD & DRINKS

16 MAP P72, C2

A small but handy shop for picking up provisions, this chain has all the essentials for a gourmet picnic. You'll find cheeses, cured meats, wines, craft beer, a few seasonal fruits, snacks and a tempting antipasti counter. (Via Roma 61; 9am-7pm daily Oct-Mar, 8.30am-8.30pm Mon-Sat, to 7.30pm Sun Apr-Sep)

Top Experience 📷
Sentiero Azzurro – Monterosso to Vernazza

This popular walk follows the course of an age-old path connecting Monterosso with Vernazza. Short but steep (in parts), the trail has fabulous scenery, with views over terraced vineyards and olive groves, steep mountains fronting azure seas, and two pastel-hued story-book villages. If you have time for just one walk in Cinque Terre, make it this one.

Getting There

Take the train to Monterosso station. From there it's all on foot to Vernazza.

Admission with Cinque Terre card (p90).

❶ Monterosso

To reach the trail, exit Monterosso train station and turn left. You'll pass through the shared pedestrian-car tunnel leading to the old part of town. After the tunnel, stick to the main road that follows along the beach. Keep following this uphill as it narrows and leads you right along the water's edge. Even before you reach the official start of the trail, you'll have some fine views – just remember to turn around to check out the picture-perfect view of the village nestled between beach and the undulating green hills high above town.

❷ Stairs & Vineyards

About 400m from town, you'll reach the staffed entrance to the trail, where you'll need to purchase a trekking pass (cash only) if you haven't already. The ascent begins gently enough, passing by vineyards to right and left, with periodic lookouts back to Monterosso. Soon, the climbing will begin in earnest as you tackle many flights of steps (there are over 500 throughout the walk). Keep an eye out for the sign announcing Vétua, a small family-run vineyard of just 6000 square metres. Here Bosco, Albarola and Vermentino are cultivated to create classic varieties of Cinque Terre DOC white wine. Aside from grapes, Vétua also grows lemons, artichokes, capers and herbs – all produced sustainably.

❸ Nature's Bounty

As you continue uphill, you'll soon realise how lush the landscape becomes as you leave the coast behind and wind your way inland. You'll pass moss-covered stone walls, thick blooms of wisteria and trickling steams crisscrossing the path – with the occasional stone bridge above faster flowing waters. Inland views reveal a fertile valley with a patchwork of farms hemmed in by rolling green hills rising above. You'll pass

★ Top Tips

○ Although only a 3.4km walk, this trail is strenuous, with some long ascents (up many stairs).

○ Wear good walking shoes as the path can be slippery in places from loose rocks or trickling streams; avoid hiking during bad weather (check the forecast before setting out).

○ Be sure to bring water (there's none along the way) and wear a hat and sunscreen, as there isn't any shade on some parts of the walk.

✕ Take a Break

Before hitting the trail, pick up some oven-baked snacks from Il Massimo della Focaccia (p73).

At walk's end, treat yourself to a gelato in Vernazza at the harbourside Il Porticciolo (p91).

right beside fields of olive trees and figs, strands of wildflowers and the odd cactus, plus blackberry brambles edging along the path.

❹ The Sea

Around the halfway point, the trail winds its way back to the coast, and you'll be greeted with dramatic views over the seaside. You'll hear the crashing waves and feel the sea breezes as you peer over the Mediterranean greenery. In contrast to the manicured lands you've just past through, the landscape here is wild and untouched with a view stretching far off into the distance of the steep mountainsides that intersect with the foaming waters surrounding the wave-battered shore. In parts, the drop-off is fairly straight down, so watch your footing

(keep children close if hiking with little ones).

❺ Village Views

The worst of the climbing is now behind you, with only a few gentle ups and downs over the rest of the walk. This will allow you to enjoy the mesmerising perspective of Vernazza, which comes in and out of view as you follow the winding cliff-side trail. At first glance the seaside village seems like something from a fable: tiny pastel-coloured buildings nestled amid the imposing mountainsides rising above at near vertical angles. The details come more into focus as you round the final bend: the harbourfront buildings standing tightly together, with the geometric block of a medieval tower set on the sea cliff just behind them. The tiny beach, watched over by the

belltower of the church, sits beside the small waterfront plaza, hardly visible beneath the yellow, red, blue and green umbrellas of the piazza's alfresco restaurants and cafes. And behind the waterfront, terraced vineyards rise steeply beyond the village.

❻ Vernazza

Nearing the village (pictured p78), you'll see once again the culti-vated fields that are so deeply a part of Cinque Terre's past. Olive groves, vineyards, lemon trees and vegetable gardens grow just beyond the rock walls skirting the trail. You might hear the tolling of church bells and the clamour of children frolicking in the water, and spot more details of village life: laundry lines flapping in the breeze beneath dark-green shutters thrown open to let in the fresh sea breezes. Soon you'll pass the ticket booth for Monterosso-bound hikers, and arrive at eye level with the cupola of Santa Margherita d'Antiochia. From here, just above the church, you'll have a picture-perfect panorama of Vernazza – indeed even those who don't make the hike come up to this viewpoint for the inspiring perspective.

Early Start

Being one of the few coastal trails open between villages, this walk gets frustratingly crowded. Going can be slow in parts, as you wait on the most narrow sections for people coming toward you to pass. To avoid the worst of the crowds, go very early in the morning; at the very least avoid being out when the trails are busiest, which is from roughly 10am until 4pm.

❼ The Harbour

After passing the church, the path turns into Via Ettore Vernazza. For the perfect cap to the walk, take the first set of stairs leading down to the right. These put you right onto the waterfront Piazza Guglielmo Marconi, where you can have a drink or a meal, or refresh over some gelato while sitting on the breakwall and taking in one of Cinque Terre's most vibrant set-tings. Be sure to take a peak inside the Chiesa di Santa Margherita d'Antiochia (p89), a few steps from the waterfront. The atmospheric Ligurian-Gothic church is one of the finest in Cinque Terre.

Explore ◈
Vernazza

*Vernazza's small harbour – the only secure land-
ing point on the Cinque Terre coast – guards what
is perhaps the quaintest, and steepest, of the five
villages. Lined with little cafes, a main cobbled street
(Via Roma) links seaside Piazza Marconi with the train
station. Side streets lead to the village's trademark
Genoa-style carurgi (narrow streets), where sea views
pop at every turn.*

The Short List

○ **Vernazza Harbour (p84)** *Watching the day unfold
while taking in the boats, the beach and the captivating
coastline.*

○ **Chiesa di Santa Margherita d'Antiochia (p89)**
*Stepping back in time a few centuries amid Cinque
Terre's most atmospheric church.*

○ **Belforte (p89)** *Enjoying Vernazza's best cooking
while watching the sunset from inside an 11th-century
fortification.*

○ **Gocce di Byron (p92)** *Discovering intriguing fragrances inspired by Liguria's enchanting landscapes.*

○ **Burgus Bar (p91)** *Relaxing with a glass of Cinque
Terre's finest while taking in the afternoon view over
the seaside Piazza Marconi.*

Getting There & Around

🚃 Vernazza is on the main train line for the Trenitalia Cinque
Terre Express trains.

Vernazza Map on p88

Verazza village ANIBAL TREJO / SHUTTERSTOCK ©

Top Sight 📷
Vernazza Harbour

Cinque Terre's only natural harbour has breath-taking views out over the water, and provides the best open-air amusement in Vernazza. Here you can bask on a tiny beach, head off on a boat trip, or just linger over the day's fresh catch and a glass of Italy's finest at one of the alfresco restaurants facing the water's edge.

◎ **MAP P88, C2**

Off Via Visconti

Piazza Marconi

The epicentre of village life revolves around this picturesque waterfront square. On clear days, the terrace restaurants and cafes provide a magnificent setting for a fresh seafood meal or an afternoon cocktail. You'll also find some of Vernazza's best gelato here, which you can take to the seawall fringing the piazza.

The Beach

On warm summer days, this tiny beach at the end of the piazza draws sunbathers to the water's edge. Normally, the waters are fairly calm here, with boats bobbing just offshore and children splashing about in the cool sea. You can also rent boats (kayaks, motorboats) and arrange excursions from here.

Swimming & Lounging

For more action in the harbour, you can follow the narrow waterside lane past the church. Here, you can lounge on the flat rocks at the water's edge or float idly while trains glide past, above the high stone wall fringing the lapping waves.

Via Visconti

The harbour anchors the western end of Via Visconti, the main street coursing through Vernazza. This vibrant cobblestone lane provides enticements of all sorts, including great street food – gelato, focaccia slices, cones of fried seafood – which is best enjoyed back on the waterfront. As the street continues along (changing names to Via Roma), you'll also find one-of-a-kind shops selling everything from locally produced perfumes to stylish beachwear.

★ Top Tips

o Go early in the morning to see the harbour at its most serene.

o Book a restaurant table for sunset. It's a magical time to be out facing the water.

o Tie in your visit with a boat tour for a look at the magnificent coastal scenery from a Mediterranean vantage point.

✕ Take a Break

Burgus Bar (p91) is an easygoing spot where you can enjoy excellent wines and cocktails while taking in village life from the tables out front.

Nothing beats gelato on the waterfront on a sunny day, particularly the high-quality flavours served at Il Porticciolo (p91).

Walking Tour 🥾

Vernazza

This scenic jaunt around Vernazza takes you past historic buildings, along the village's bustling main drag and up into the peaceful back lanes above the centre. You'll also pass numerous spots for photos here, with views over the harbour, the village and the rugged coastline outside of town. To beat the day-tripping crowds, go early in the morning or late in the afternoon.

Walk Facts

Start Piazzetta dei Caduti;
🚉 Vernazza

End Via E Vernazza;
🚉 Vernazza

Length 1.5km; one to two hours

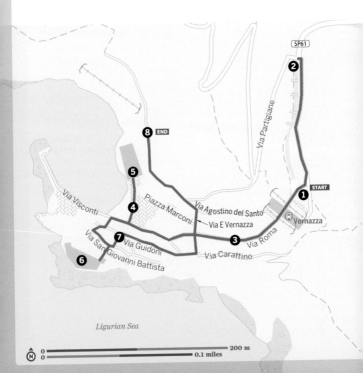

❶ Piazzetta dei Caduti

Just uphill from the train station, the tiny **Piazzetta dei Caduti** gathers a mix of young families and old-timers seeking a reprieve from the busyness down by the harbour. In one corner of the plaza is a monument dedicated to victims of the world wars, with names inscribed on a marble plaque. Note also the millstone, evidence of an old water mill once located nearby.

❷ Torrente Vernazzola

Keep strolling uphill to reach the gently flowing **Torrente Vernazzola**. This stream was once much wider and was a gathering spot for locals who did their washing on the riverbank. Today, it's fringed by modern apartment blocks, with several tiny bridges over the stream.

❸ Via Roma

Descend into the heart of Vernazza along **Via Roma**, a winding lane packed with shops, restaurants and cafes. Just past the train station, a poster shows the devastation wrought by floods in October 2011. The small stone chapel further along is dedicated to Santa Marta.

❹ Vernazza Waterfront

At the end of Via Roma, you'll reach an open **plaza** flanked by restaurants. Outdoor tables just above the water's edge enjoy picture-perfect views of boats bobbing in the harbour, against rolling green hills flanking the seaside.

❺ Chiesa di Santa Margherita d'Antiochia

Cross the plaza and take the stairs up to the striking Ligurian-Gothic **Chiesa di Santa Margherita d'Antiochia** (p89), which dates back to the 14th century. The stone walls and narrow windows create an austere though undeniably atmospheric interior.

❻ Castello Doria

Ascend the staircase to the left and follow the signs to **Castello Doria** (p89). This imposing tower once helped protect the city against seaside invasions in the Middle Ages. Head up top for a striking view over Vernazza.

❼ Via Guidoni

Take the narrow lane **Via Guidoni** that parallels Via Roma. Here you'll have a glimpse of old-school Vernazza, with tightly packed dwellings, window-box flowers and laundry lines flapping overhead.

❽ Lookout

As you round a narrow bend, take the steps leading down, cross Via Roma and continue up the stairs (Via E Vernazza) on the opposite side of the main drag. Keep following this path, and you'll reach a **lookout** above the church, offering a fine view over the harbour and the terraced vineyards just out of town.

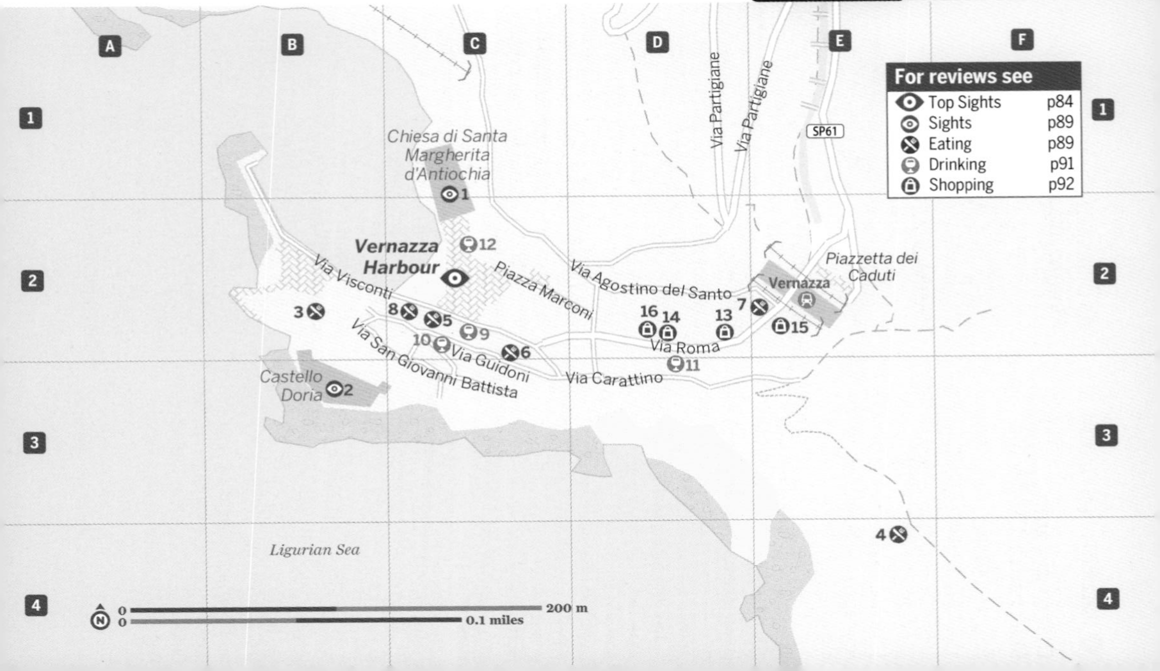

Vernazza

For reviews see

◉	Top Sights	p84
⊙	Sights	p89
⊗	Eating	p89
🍸	Drinking	p91
🛍	Shopping	p92

Chiesa di Santa Margherita d'Antiochia

⊙1

Via Partigiane

Via Partigiane

SP61

Piazzetta dei Caduti

Vernazza

Ⓚ

🛍15

7 ⊗

13 ⊙

14 16
🍸 🛍

Via Agostino del Santo

Via Roma

⊙11

Via Carattino

⊙12

Piazza Marconi

Vernazza Harbour ◉

8 ⊗

⊗5

🍸9

⊗6

Via Visconti

10 🍸

Via Guidoni

Via San Giovanni Battista

3 ⊗

Castello Doria

⊙2

Ligurian Sea

4 ⊗

0 ────── 200 m
0 ────── 0.1 miles

Ⓝ

Sights

Chiesa di Santa Margherita d'Antiochia CHURCH

1 ⊙ MAP P88, C1

The waterfront is framed by this little Ligurian-Gothic church, built on a small seafront promontory in 1318 on the site of an 11th-century Romanesque building. According to legend, the church was constructed here after a box containing the bones of St Margaret washed up on a nearby beach. It is notable for its unusual 40m-tall octagonal tower topped with a dome.

Inside, the church contains several 17th-century paintings, and a wooden crucifix attributed to Anton Maria Maragliano. The views through the narrow arched windows are outstanding. (Piazza Matteotti)

Castello Doria CASTLE

2 ⊙ MAP P88, B3

This castle, which is the oldest surviving fortification in Cinque Terre, commands superb views. Dating to around 1000, it's now largely a ruin except for the circular tower located in the centre of the esplanade. To get there, head up the steep, narrow staircase located by the harbour. (Off Via Guidoni; €1.50; ⊙10am-9pm May-Aug, to 7pm Sep-Apr)

Santuario della Madonna di Reggio

From underneath Vernazza's railway bridge, follow trail 508 up numerous flights of steps and past 14 sculpted Stations of the Cross to an 11th-century chapel with a Romanesque facade. It's approximately a 45-minute walk.

Eating

Belforte SEAFOOD €€€

3 ⊗ MAP P88, B2

A Vernazza classic for more than 50 years, Belforte serves beautifully prepared seafood dishes in an 11th-century castle. You can dine in the atmospheric stone-walled interior or enjoy the breezy views from one of the terraces. The prices are steep, but most diners rate the experience highly. Reserve ahead. (☑0187 81 22 22; www.ristorante belforte.it; Via Guidoni 42; meals €35-55; ⊙noon-3pm & 7-10pm Wed-Mon)

La Torre SEAFOOD €€

4 ⊗ MAP P88, E4

Tucked along a hillside pathway just outside the centre, La Torre serves Genoese-style *trofie al pesto* (a pasta with pesto), seafood spaghetti, stuffed mussels and other classic fare, though the real attraction is the views from the long terrace. It's also a prime spot for a sunset cocktail. Cash only.

Cinque Terre Card

If you plan to hike between villages, the best way to get around Cinque Terre is with a Cinque Terre card.

Two versions of the card are available: with or without train travel. Both include unlimited use of walking paths and electric village buses, as well as cultural exhibitions. The basic one-/two-day card for those aged over four years costs €7.50/14.50. With unlimited train trips between the towns, the card costs €16/29. A one-day family card for two adults and two children (under 12) costs €42/20 with/without train travel.

Both versions of the card are sold at all Cinque Terre park information offices and each of Cinque Terre's train stations. You can also purchase trail admission at each of the trailheads (cash only).

Because the tables are located entirely outdoors, La Torre closes on bad weather days. (☑331 883 6610; Via Carattino 64; meals €35-40; ⏱11am-10pm)

Gambero Rosso   SEAFOOD €€

5 ✕ MAP P88, C2

If you've been subsisting on focaccia, Gambero's house specials – *tegame di Vernazza* (anchovies with baked potatoes and tomatoes), grilled rock octopus or stuffed mussels – will really hit the spot; and the fresh fish baked in sea salt is outstanding. It tastes all the better in the excellent waterfront location. Bookings recommended. (☑0187 81 22 65; www.ristorantegamberorosso.net; Piazza Marconi 7; meals €35-45; ⏱noon-3pm & 7-10pm Fri-Wed)

Gianni Franzi   SEAFOOD €€

6 ✕ MAP P88, C2

Traditional Cinque Terre seafood (mussels, seafood ravioli and lemon anchovies) has been served up in this harbourside trattoria since the 1960s. When it comes to seafood this fresh, if it's not broken, don't fix it. The outdoor tables make a magnificent setting to relax just about any time of day. (☑0187 81 22 28; www.giannifranzi.it; Piazza Matteotti 5; meals €30-45; ⏱8am-11pm Thu-Tue mid-Mar–early Jan)

Blue Marlin   CAFE €

7 ✕ MAP P88, E2

With outdoor tables situated on the main drag and a lively soundtrack, Blue Marlin draws a steady stream of locals and visitors throughout the day. Stop in for flaky croissants, scrambled eggs and cappuccinos in the morning, or visit later in the day for flavour-packed focaccia, pizzas and daily seafood specials – like spaghetti with clams or black taglierini with swordfish. (Via Roma 47; light meals €5-10, daily specials €9-14; ⏱7am-midnight Thu-Tue)

Il Porticciolo

GELATO €

8 ✖ MAP P88, C2

In a perfect location on the waterfront, Il Porticciolo whips up heavenly perfection in its all-natural gelato. Indulge in fruit flavours such as strawberry, lemon (locally sourced) or green apple, or opt for Greek yoghurt served with local honey, hazelnut or *ambrogio* (a combination of nuts, cream and chocolate). (www.facebook.com/gelateriailporticciolo; Piazza Marconi 12; gelato from €2.50; ⏱11.30am-11pm)

Seafood plate, Gambero Rosso

Drinking

Burgus Bar

WINE BAR

9 🍷 MAP P88, C2

A charming little hole-in-the-wall, with only a couple of ringside benches looking over Piazza Marconi to the little beach, this neighbourhood bar serves up glasses of the fragrant, ethereal mix of local Albarola, Bosco and Vermentino grapes that is Cinque Terre DOC. It also does breakfast pastries, sandwiches and *aperitivo*, and stocks a range of local produce to take away. (Piazza Marconi 4; ⏱9.30am-9pm Mar-May, to midnight Jun-Oct)

Monkey Artpub

BAR

10 🍷 MAP P88, C2

Hidden down a narrow lane just a few steps off the harbour, Monkey Artpub is an atmospheric drinking den that has dark stone walls, an artfully lit shelf of libations and quality Baladin on draught. The friendly owner speaks excellent English, and is happy to share tips on the area. (Via Guidoni 11; ⏱11am-11pm)

5 Terre Bistrot

WINE BAR

11 🍷 MAP P88, D3

Slightly concealed above the chapel along Vernazza's main street, this small wine shop and bar is a fine place to sample some of Cinque Terre's finest. You can enjoy local wines and snacks along with quality beers such as

Escaping the Crowds

Timing Your Visit

Cinque Terre's busiest months are May through September, when the villages get jam-packed with tourists. If you come during this time, try to do your exploring early or late in the day, after the day trippers have gone. During midday, plan some downtime on a beach outside of Cinque Terre or do a private tour (boating, kayaking, snorkelling) to escape the crowds.

Evening Hours

Even in the height of summer, things can be remarkably calm around sundown when the thicker crowds have dispersed. Take advantage of warm summer evenings for long meals – just be sure to reserve ahead. Trains run until around 11.30pm or midnight, so it's not a problem basing yourself in nearby La Spezia or Levanto, and returning late in the evening. Just keep in mind that trains run only every hour or so after about 7.30pm.

Weihenstephaner at the outdoor tables located in front of the bar. (📞0187 882 10 84; Via Roma 44; ⏲11am-10pm)

Ananasso Bar   BAR

12 🚏 MAP P88, C2

Get here early to score a seat on the terrace at this youthful, easygoing cafe, with its yellow-umbrella-shaded tables perched above Vernazza's tiny beach. Aside from coffee and cocktails, Ananasso Bar also serves inexpensive snacks – dishes such as stuffed focaccia, pizzas, salads and the like. (www.facebook.com/ananasso5terre; Piazza Marconi; ⏲8am-11pm)

Shopping

Gocce di Byron   PERFUME

13 🔒 MAP P88, D2

Cinque Terre's lemon trees, vineyards and seashore are among the inspirations for the alluring fragrances that are created by the locally based perfume maker. At this sunny little shop, you can browse the five signature scents, each named after Cinque Terre places (like Guvano, made of white musk and sandalwood). It also sells skincare products, scented candles and diffusers. (www.goccedibyron.it; Via Roma 35; ⏲10.30am-7pm daily Apr-Oct, to 9pm Jun-Aug)

Enoteca Sciacchetrà

Bottega d'Arte
ART

14 🔒 MAP P88, D2

Hidden behind a small facade, Bottega d'Arte sells the paintings of Antonio Greco, who spent his childhood in Vernazza. His works of seascapes and village scenes evoke the magic of Cinque Terre. The other half of Bottega d'Arte is devoted to jewellery made from vintage pieces sourced from markets around Italy. (www.cinqueterreart. com; Via Roma 21; ◷10.30am-7pm)

Il Talismano
FASHION & ACCESSORIES

15 🔒 MAP P88, E2

A fabulous place to browse, this atmospheric shop sells beautiful jewellery (horn bracelets, vintage silver earrings, amber necklaces), bags made from African textiles, and other unique wares sourced from the owner's extensive travels. You'll also find high-quality leather products (wallets, satchels, handbags) made in Italy and 100% cashmere scarves from Nepal. (📞0187 02 81 75; www.facebook. com/iltalismanoofficial; Via Roma 70; ◷10am-10.30pm Jul & Aug, to 8.30pm Jun, Sep & Oct, to 6pm Mar-May)

Enoteca Sciacchetrà
FOOD & DRINKS

16 🔒 MAP P88, D2

Pick up a fine bottle of Nebbiolo or Montepulciano at this wine shop on the main drag. You'll also find Sciacchetrà (dessert wine local to Cinque Terre), truffle-infused olive oils, Genoese pesto, lemon candies, olive-wood mortars and pestles, and liqueurs. (Via Roma 19; ◷10am-7pm)

Top Experience 📷
Aquatic Adventures

There are many ways to experience Cinque Terre's dramatic setting – whether on a ferry zipping between villages, on a private boat tour, or on a slow-paced kayak excursion. You can also indulge in the life aquatic by going for a swim, spending the day on an island or simply enjoying the scenery from one of the beaches in the area.

Parco Nazionale Offices

www.parconazionale
5terre.it

Provides information about water activities.

Offices located in all Cinque Terre train stations.

🕐 8am-8pm summer, 8.30am-12.30pm & 1-5.30pm winter

Ferries

One of the easiest ways to get out on the water is to hop on a ferry. Apart from Corniglia, ferry boats call at every village in Cinque Terre. There are also ferries to Portofino and Porto Venere, with onward connections to Lerici and Tellaro. While crowded in summer, these boats offer fabulous views along the coastline, taking in the meandering hillsides, wave-battered shores and the terraced vineyards edging above each Cinque Terre village.

Tours & Boat Hire

There are various organised tours that offer a more small-group experience if you want to take in the coastline without all of the crowds. You can also hire a boat and captain to explore at your own leisure, stopping at places like Guvano Beach (p96) and **acqua pendente** – a sparkling waterfall located between Vernazza and Monterosso. Outfitters such as **Crazy Boat Cinque Terre** (☎ 328 9365595; www.crazyboatcinqueterre. com) charge around €100 per hour, taking up to seven passengers.

Kayaking

The coastline is ripe for exploring on a paddling trip. You can hire kayaks from Monterosso, Vernazza, Manarola or Riomaggiore. Avoid going when the seas are rough. And if you're not confident in your skills, you're better off booking a tour. Reputable agencies like **Arbaspàa** (☎ 0187 76 00 83; www.arbaspaa.com; Via Discovolo 252; 👤) lead half- and full-day tours departing from Monterosso, with stops for snorkelling and swimming at wild beaches.

Beaches & Swimming Spots

Though not known for its beaches, the Cinque Terre region has some fine stretches of shoreline nearby. In the towns themselves,

★ Top Tips

○ Ferries can get quite crowded during the busy summer months. Set off early to avoid the worst of the crowds.

○ A sunset kayaking tour is a great way to end the day.

○ Hiking around the island of Palmaria is a great way to experience the beauty of the region without the crowds.

○ In the summer, you can reach Cinque Terre by boat from other destinations in Liguria, including Sestri Levante, Portofino and Genoa.

✗ Take a Break

A memorable setting for an alfresco drink and bite is A Pié de Mà (p129) in Riomaggiore.

You'll find excellent gelato at any of Cinque Terre's villages, but Il Porticciolo (p91) in Vernazza has an unbeatable waterfront location.

Monterosso has the only proper stretch of beach. Heading out of the train station, you'll find appealing stretches of shore to right or left – with free sections sandwiched between admission-only beach clubs.

Vernazza has a tiny beach that makes a fine spot for cooling off when the waves aren't too rough. There's also a small rocky swimming area just past the church of Santa Margherita di Antiocha. Hilltop **Corniglia** also has a swimming spot – a rocky cove reached by heading down the lane off the main plaza. The rocky waterfront below Corniglia's train station attracts a few sunbathers, though it's not particularly scenic.

In **Manarola**, young daredevils leap from the rocks into the tiny harbour (p113); on calm days, the waters here are like a swimming pool (a ladder allows access). You can also follow the path which wraps around Punta Bonfiglio to another swimming spot just off a boat ramp. **Riomaggiore**'s rocky beach (p127) feels secreted from the village and is one of the most scenic in the area. Reach it by following the water's edge past the ferry dock then along a ledge to a small rocky expanse flanked by lush hillsides cascading down to the seashore. Wherever you go, set out early to beat the crowds, or come later in the day when the day trippers have departed.

Once a famed destination for nudists, **Guvano Beach** is a peaceful stretch of pebbled shoreline nestled in a scenic cove roughly halfway between Corniglia and Vernazza. It was once easier to access via an

Manarola

abandoned railway tunnel from Corniglia. Unfortunately, landslides have made the tunnel no longer passable and these days mostly private boats make the trip here. On calm days, it makes a fine destination for kayakers setting out from Vernazza.

Outside of the Cinque Terre villages, appealing beaches lie to the north and south. A short train ride from Monterosso, **Levanto** has a long, wide beach (p62) that's all sand. Take your pick of public or private beach access. It's also a great setting for walking, running and cycling, with a greenway that heads to Bonassola (and Framura beyond) along a former railway line.

Harder to reach, **San Terenzo** and **Lerici** (p138) lie on the eastern shores of the Gulf of La Spezia. Here you'll find sparkling beaches (mostly sand, with some stones beyond the shallowest water) that draw mostly Italian holidaymakers in the summer. Get there by ferry from Cinque Terre or by train to La Spezia and a connecting bus from there.

Islands

Palmaria

The largest island of the Italian Riviera, Palmaria is mostly undeveloped (it's home to around 50 residents) and lies just a short ferry ride from Porto Venere. Set with towering cliffs, picturesque coves and rocky beaches, the 1.9-sq-km Palmaria makes a fascinating destination for a day trip. There are several well-maintained hiking trails on the island, including the 510, which circles the island and takes you up high slopes, through Mediterranean forest and past pristine shorelines on a moderately difficult three-hour walk. hour walk. Ferries run every 30 minutes during summer (and every couple of hours off season) from Porto Venere to Punta Secca (€5, five minutes).

Tino & Tinetto

Two tiny islands hiding behind Palmaria provide a window into the Italian Riviera's distant past. Tino, the bigger of the two has towering sea cliffs and a luxuriant appearance thanks to its forests of pine and holm oak. A Benedictine monastery was founded here in the Middle Ages, though monastic orders were present here even earlier. According to legend, Friar Venerio lived on the island in the 7th century and used to light fires at the highest point on the island as a guide to mariners. (He was later coronated and became the patron saint of lighthouse keepers.) Nowadays, a lighthouse stands where presumably the monk kept the fires burning. Tiny Tinetto contains the ruins of a 6th-century oratory; it's also home to a rare species of endemic lizard.

Boat trips from Porto Venere provide fine views of Tino and Tinetto as well as Palmaria.

Top Experience 📷
Sentiero Azzurro – Vernazza to Corniglia

The walk from Vernazza to Corniglia takes you along sea cliffs, through Mediterranean bush and along fields that have been cultivated since the Middle Ages. While short, this trail involves a fair bit of climbing, though the rewards up top are unforgettable. Mesmerising views unfold on every turn, with sweeping panoramas over the jagged mountainscapes that descend precipitously to the shoreline.

Getting There

Take the train to Vernazza. Head downhill towards the waterfront to find the start of the walk.

Admission with Cinque Terre card (p90)

❶ Vernazza

You'll find the start of this walk by heading toward the waterfront along Via Roma, and taking the first left after the pharmacy. Look for the small sign with red arrows labelled 'Sentiero per Corniglia' on the wall. Head up the steps and follow this *caruggi* (narrow street) as it winds up through the back parts of town. Veer left up the stairs at the first T-intersection; after another 200m you'll see a well-worn stone staircase up to the right, with a 'Corniglia' sign pointing the way beside red-and-white blaze (these are used everywhere in Cinque Terre as trail markers).

❷ Picture-Perfect Panorama

The stairs take you up to a lookout with a jaw-dropping view over Vernazza. Just past a cylindrical stone building, you'll see just how fragile this village appears. Much of the town lies atop a craggy peninsula that stretches fingerlike into the sea. From here, you can peer over wildflowers and cacti clinging to the hillside just below your feet, down to the tiny beach below the cliffs. The iconic features of Vernazza appear most dramatic in the early or afternoon light – the old medieval tower at the edge of the sea that served as a lookout for invaders, the shimmering cupola over Cinque Terre's prettiest church, and the town's curving breakwall protecting its harbour from crashing waves (which can be quite violent during storms).

❸ Abandoned Terraces

Continuing on the path, you'll shortly reach the checkpoint to hike the Sentierro Azzurro, where you can purchase your ticket if you haven't already. The checkpoint also lies near the trailhead to 507 (admission free), which connects to the Alta Via delle Cinque Terre (AV5T), the 38km path that runs high above the villages between Levanto in the north and Porto

★ Top Tips

o As with every other walk in the heavily visited Cinque Terre, aim to get on the trail early to avoid the crowds. Sunrise is a great time to experience the unblemished beauty of this coastline.

o Most travellers complete the 4km trail in around 90 minutes.

o Coming from Vernazza, you'll ascend just over 280m during the course of the walk. If you want to cut out a bit of the climb, start in Corniglia, which is less steep than on the Vernazza side.

✕ Take a Break

After arriving in Corniglia, reward yourself with a refreshing treat at Alberto Gelateria (p107).

Just before arriving in Corniglia, you can stop for a snack on the trail at Il Gabbiano (p101).

Venere in the south, with multiple access trails at each of the villages along the way. The walk starts off with gentle ascents, following the cliff edge along the sea with superb views at every turn. You'll start out above the open train tracks. Around 500m up the track, you'll begin climbing up uneven stone steps which zigzag past olive trees and stretches of bushy forest. You'll also pass terraced gardens that have long since been abandoned.

4 Mediterranean Wilderness

The path is compacted dirt or flat stones in places, with plenty of stairs throughout. Along the cliffs, wooden railings provide added protection, but the trail suffers significant wear and tear during the rainy months. Soon, you'll reach a wild part of the coast with views of densely forested slopes of distinct Mediterranean vegetation stretching ahead, and the cliffs to your right thick with Indian fig opuntia and agave plants.

5 A Sleepy Settlement

Around the midpoint of your journey (some 2km from Corniglia), you'll pass the hamlet of **Prevo** off to your left. According to tradition, the tiny settlement was founded in the 16th century by families of mountain shepherds who migrated here in the winters to shelter with their flocks. Protected by dry stone walls, the terraces here nurture vegetable gardens, lemon and pomegranate trees, as well as cherries and quince.

6 Islands in the Mist

Slow down to admire the view here, as you're standing on one of the

highest points of the Sentiero Azzurro at an elevation of 208m. On clear days, you have a fine vantage point over the distant islands of Corsica, Elba, Gorgona and Capraia. You'll also have a spectacular view of Corniglia, which resembles a toy village from this height – a jumble of pastel-coloured buildings huddling tightly together atop the steep seemingly vertical cliffs above the swirling sea. You'll see the terraced gardens just behind the village; while further along the coastline you can just make out the village of Manarola.

❼ Clifftop Refreshment

One of the only places where you'll find refreshment on the Sentiero Azzurro, sits alongside the trail (on the Mediterranean side) in Prevo. **Il Gabbiano** (snacks from €4; ⏰9am-6pm) serves up cold drinks (smoothies, iced coffees, *granite*) as well as *panini* and other snacks. Perched right over the cliff, the shaded outdoor tables have magnificent views. If you really fall for the setting, there's also a guesthouse a few steps away – the Heart of Cinque Terre (aka Leo's Lodge).

❽ Pastoral Landscapes

Arriving in Corniglia is quite a different experience from arriving at any other Cinque Terre village. You'll likely hear a few crowing roosters as you near the village,

Rocky Shoreline

At the trip's end, you can rejuvenate in the bracing waters off Corniglia's little-known rocky waterfront – though keep in mind you'll have a short but steep climb back to town. To get there, take Via Fieschi and turn right just before you reach the main piazza. Follow this down to the rocky shoreline. Don't forget to bring your swimsuit (and a towel!).

barking dogs and the ever-present sound of twittering birds, with the sounds carrying across the valley. There's also a more decidedly pastoral air to the surroundings, with the cultivated fields growing up right to the edge of the settlement.

❾ Corniglia

The knee-killing descent begins at the outskirts of town, as you negotiate a seemingly endless stretch of stairs. After this you'll cross several bridges over the mountain streams before reaching the main road into town. Cross the pavement and look for the connecting path, which continues a few metres up on the left. You'll wind your way into the village past vineyards to right and left. Eventually, you'll reach the top of Via Fieschi, near the steps of the Chiesa di San Pietro. Turn right onto this lane, which will lead into the heart of tiny Corniglia (pictured p98).

Explore ⊛

Corniglia

Corniglia is the 'quiet' middle village that sits atop a 100m-high rocky promontory surrounded by vineyards. It is the only Cinque Terre settlement with no direct sea access, although steep steps lead down to a rocky cove. Narrow alleys and colourfully painted four-storey houses characterise the ancient core, a timeless streetscape that was namechecked in Boccaccio's Decameron.

The Short List

○ **Belvedere di Santa Maria (p109)** *Taking in the magnificent clifftop view of the four other Cinque Terre villages.*

○ **Chiesa San Pietro (p107)** *Admiring the fine artisanship inside Corniglia's 14th-century church.*

○ **Santuario della Madonna delle Grazie (p107)** *Climbing up past forested hillsides to the settlement of San Bernardino for a stunning coastal panorama.*

○ **Alberto Gelateria (p107)** *Tasting some of Liguria's best gelato made from locally sourced ingredients.*

○ **La Scuna (p108)** *Toasting the sunset while drinking craft brews and munching on flavour-packed appetisers.*

Getting There & Around

🚆 The village is on the main train line for the Trenitalia Cinque Terre Express trains. From the station, it's a steep ascent to the village via a 377-step brick stairway; a shuttle bus (€2.50) also meets the train.

Corniglia Map on p106

Corniglia terraced landscape NOEMI SANTUCCI / EYEEM / GETTY IMAGES ©

Walking Tour 🥾

Corniglia

Though tiny in size, Corniglia has some memorable attractions that make it well worth the steep climb up from the train station. This easy jaunt through town takes in centuries-old churches, shady plazas and magnificent views (where you can see all the Cinque Terre villages on clear days), plus some famous gelato along the way.

Walk Facts

Start Piazzetta Ciapara; 🚇 Corniglia

End Belvedere di Santa Maria; 🚇 Corniglia

Length 400m; one hour

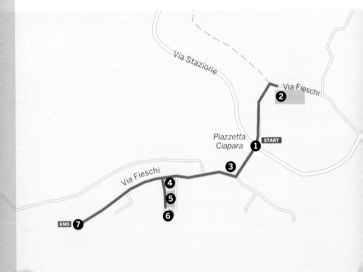

❶ Piazzetta Ciapara

Begin the day at the tiny **Piazzetta Ciapara** at the entrance to the village. While most travellers pass quickly through, it's a good place to slow down and take in the pace of village life. There are a few shaded benches, a couple of small markets for refreshments, and an old wine press in the centre of the square – a remnant of Corniglia's once pivotal wine industry.

❷ Chiesa San Pietro

Take the little lane leading uphill to reach the small 14th-century **church of St Peter** (p107). The grey stone facade looks a little less imposing thanks to the delicate Carrara-marble rose window and the diminutive statue of St Peter over the entrance. The interior is awash with baroque finery, including a finely crafted altarpiece and 18th-century paintings.

❸ Alberto Gelateria

Head back to the square and take the narrow lane (Corniglia's main street) leading into the heart of the village. It's a short stroll to **Alberto Gelateria** (p107), home to some of Cinque Terre's best gelato. Go for flavours like basil and lemon, made of ingredients sourced right from Corniglia's hillsides.

❹ Largo Taragio

From here, it's a pleasant saunter past shops and restaurants down to the leafy **Largo Taragio**, which is the epicentre of Corniglia. Cafe tables provide prime spots for people-watching. In the centre of the square stands a small memorial, dedicated to fallen soldiers in WWI.

❺ Oratory

Take the steps up to the small **oratory** dedicated to both St Catherine and the Virgin Mary. The simple chapel has a rather austere interior apart from several 18th-century paintings and a ceiling fresco depicting the martyrdom of St Catherine (note the spoked wheels, which were part of her tortures according to tradition).

❻ Viewpoint

Behind the oratory is a small plaza of sorts, used by local children as a soccer pitch. There is a fine **viewpoint** here overlooking a sweep of coastline to the southeast, verdant hills arcing down towards waterside Manarola.

❼ Belvedere di Santa Maria

Via Fieschi ends another 80m further at Corniglia's most impressive lookout, **Belvedere di Santa Maria** (p109). You'll have a magnificent 180-degree view along the coast, from the southernmost Cinque Terre village of Riomaggiore up to the forest-covered peninsula of Punta Mesco in the northwest.

Corniglia

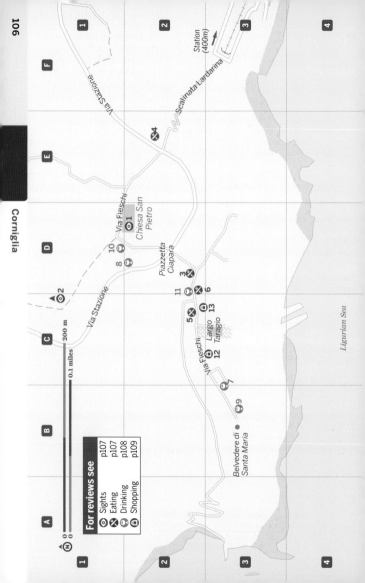

0   200 m
0   0.1 miles

For reviews see
⊙⊗ Sights	p107
⊗ Eating	p107
⊙⊙ Drinking	p108
⊡ Shopping	p109

Via Stazione

Station
(400m)

Scalinata Lardarina

Via Fieschi

Chiesa San
Pietro

⊙1

⊗4

2⊙

Via Stazione

10⊙

8⊙

Piazzetta
Ciapara

3⊙

11⊙

5⊗

6⊗

Via Fieschi

12⊙

Largo
Taragio

13⊙

7⊙

9⊙

Belvedere di
Santa Maria ●

Ligurian Sea

Sights

Chiesa San Pietro   CHURCH

1 ◉ MAP P106, D2

Near the entrance to the village, the small Gothic church dedicated to St Peter has stood here since at least the 14th century (and was likely built on the site of a smaller 11th-century chapel). The grey stone facade is lightened by a lacy Carrara-marble rose window and a small statue of a key-wielding St Peter flanked by two figures above the entrance. The interior is awash with baroque finery, including a finely crafted altarpiece and 18th-century paintings. (Via Fieschi 19)

Santuario della Madonna delle Grazie   WALKING

2 ◉ MAP P106, C1

This sanctuary can be approached from either Corniglia (on trail 587) or Vernazza (trail 507); both take around an hour. The latter is considered more scenic. Branch off the Sentiero Azzurro and ascend the spectacular Sella Comeneco to the village of San Bernardino, where you'll find the church with its adored image of Madonna and Child above the altar.

Eating

Alberto Gelateria   GELATO €

3 ✖ MAP P106, D2

A Corniglia mainstay since 1999, Alberto Melandri serves some of the best gelato for miles around. Try the *basilico* (made from basil grown in his garden), *miele de Corniglia* (made of Corniglia honey), *limone* (lemon) or the perfection of simplicity in *cannella* (cinnamon). You can also opt for a *granite* (crushed ice) made from locally grown lemons. (Via Fieschi 74; gelato from €2; ⊕11am-11pm)

La Posada Ristorante   LIGURIAN €€

4 ✖ MAP P106, E2

Near the top of the stairs leading up from the train station, La Posada is one of Corniglia's most memorable settings for an alfresco meal. On a terrace fringed by olive trees and thick palms, diners tuck into plates of grilled seafood, pastas and bruschetta, while enjoying a mesmerising view over the seaside. (☏333 4542113; Via Stazione 11; meals €26-40; ⊕noon-3pm & 7-10pm Tue-Sun)

Bütiega   DELI €

5 ✖ MAP P106, C2

If you need a break from sit-down restaurant fare, pay a visit to this lovely deli and food shop. The front counter offers oven-baked veggies, made-to-order sandwiches and antipasti, and you'll find fresh seasonal produce, wines and other goodies in the back room (the one with the beautiful tiled floor). (Via Fieschi 142; meals from €10; ⊕8am-7.30pm)

Pan e Vin   ITALIAN €

6  MAP P106, D2

An all-round good option, no matter the time of day. Pan e Vin's friendly staff serve up hearty breakfasts, focaccia sandwiches, wine and appetiser specials, and a few vegan choices as well. (Via Fieschi 123; meals from €10; ⏲8am-9pm; 🖉)

Drinking

La Scuna   BAR

7 👤 MAP P106, B3

Craft beer on draught, first-rate cocktails and creative appetisers make a great combo at this surprisingly hip little spot in this most traditional of regions.

The best feature, however, is the jaw-dropping terrace, with its mesmerising views over a hill-studded stretch of coastline. (☎349 6355081; Via Fieschi 185; ⏲8.30am-11.30pm)

Terra Rossa   WINE BAR

8 👤 MAP P106, D2

Just off the road that leads down to the train station, this vine-covered terrace has pretty views over the vineyards tumbling down to the water, and specialises in local wines. Glasses run from €5 to €8, and you can also arrange flights with food pairings (from €15). Carpaccio, salads, bruschetta, anchovies and other snacks are on hand. (Via Fieschi 58; ⏲11am-10pm)

Bar Terza Terra

ELEPHOTOS / SHUTTERSTOCK ©

Bar Terza Terra
BAR

9 🚇 MAP P106, B3

The draw of this cafe is the terrace located just a bit further along, on the right. Here you can contemplate Manarola off in the distance while enjoying cocktails and appetisers. *Aperitivo* combinations (two wines with bread, pesto and anchovies from €9) are good value. Go early to score one of the few tables. (Via Fieschi 215; ⏱10am-9pm)

À Cáneva
CAFE

10 🚇 MAP P106, D1

Near the Chiesa San Pietro, this tiny bar has a few low tables and cleverly placed cushions right on the stairs of a peaceful lane. It feels like a hidden spot where you can linger over good coffee and brioches in the morning, or cocktails, focaccia and *panini* later in the day. (www.facebook.com/a.canevabar; Via Fieschi 10; ⏱7am-9pm Mon-Fri, to midnight Sat & Sun)

Enoteca Il Pirun
WINE BAR

11 🚇 MAP P106, D2

Spread across two floors of an old village house, the old-fashioned Il Pirun is named after the odd-looking wine pitcher that allows thirsty customers to drink right from a narrow spout. There's a full menu of unfussy fare: spaghetti with clams, pesto gnocchi, octopus salad – fine accompaniments to the good wine selection. (📞0187 81 23 15; Via Fieschi 51)

Belvedere di Santa Maria

Enjoy dazzling 180-degree sea views at this heart-stopping **lookout** (Map p106, B3) in hilltop Corniglia. To find it, follow Via Fieschi through the village until you eventually reach the clifftop balcony.

Shopping

Fanny Rock Bazar
ARTS & CRAFTS

12 🔒 MAP P106, C3

One of Corniglia's shop-owning pioneers, Fanny has been in business since 1997, selling brightly hued ceramics (pitchers, trays, cups, olive dishes) as well as some surprisingly collectible and fairly priced souvenirs made by her late husband Lino: photos and mini handmade guitars dedicated to hard rockers like Keith Richards and Pink Floyd. (Via Fieschi 187; ⏱10am-8pm)

Lavgon
FASHION & ACCESSORIES

13 🔒 MAP P106, C2

This Italian fashion brand markets itself as an all-female workshop of ethical fashion, and has thoughtfully designed pieces in organic cotton and other natural fibres. You'll find elegant dresses and tops, colourful jewellery that incorporates organic shapes, and silk scarves. Most pieces are designed and produced in Italy. (www.lavgon. it; Via Fieschi 45; ⏱11am-6pm)

Explore ◈

Manarola

Bequeathed with more grapevines than any other Cinque Terre village, Manarola is famous for its sweet Sciacchetrà wine. It's also awash with priceless medieval relics, supporting claims that it is the oldest of the five. The spirited locals here speak an esoteric local dialect known as Manarolese. Due to its proximity to Riomaggiore (852m away), the village is heavily trafficked, especially by Italian school parties along with the regular tourists.

The Short List

○ **Punta Bonfiglio (p115)** Admiring one of Italy's most beautiful panoramas from a promontory overlooking Manarola.

○ **Madonna delle Salute (p115)** Hiking up through vineyards past breathtaking panoramas to this historic church in Volastra.

○ **Trattoria dal Billy (p117)** Feasting on brilliantly prepared seafood on a terrace above the centre.

○ **Nessun Dorma (p118)** Drinking in the views while sipping first-rate Cinque Terre wines in the open air.

○ **L'Emporio (p119)** Browsing nautically themed artwork made by local artists.

Getting There & Around

🚆 Manarola is on the main train line for the Trenitalia Cinque Terre Express trains.

Manarola Map on p114

Manarola streetscape BRUNO - NA PROA DA VIDA / SHUTTERSTOCK ©

Walking Tour 🥾

Manarola

One of Cinque Terre's most photogenic villages, Manarola offers magnificent views from the peaceful lanes and plazas just above the centre. As you wander past key landmarks, like the Chiesa di San Lorenzo, you'll get a bit of a workout, as Manarola's main street is an uphill climb. But the lofty panoramas over the vineyards and sparkling sea are well worth the effort.

Walk Facts

Start Manarola train station; 🚉 Manarola

End Punta Bonfiglio; 🚉 Manarola

Length 1.5km; one hour

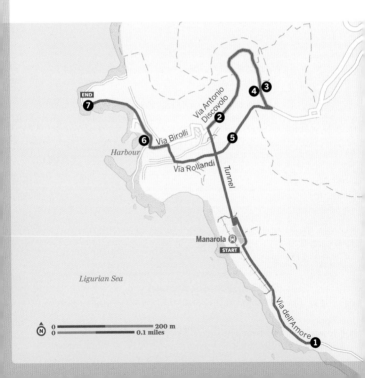

❶ Via dell'Amore

Starting from the Manarola train station, follow the path above the tracks and walk along the **Via dell'Amore**. This flat, easy path, around 1km long, once connected Manarola with Riomaggiore. Unfortunately, only 200m of it remains open following a damaging rockslide in 2012. It's worth the visit here for fine views over the crashing waves.

❷ Via Discovolo

Retrace your steps and take the pedestrian tunnel that leads to the village. As you emerge into the light, turn right. The winding lane **Via Discovolo** (named after the 20th-century Italian painter Antonio Discovolo) is the commercial artery of Manarola. Food shops, clothing stores and snack stands jockey for attention as locals and tourists wander past.

❸ Chiesa di San Lorenzo

It's a steady uphill climb as you follow the sharp curve in the road. Shortly after the bend you'll reach the **Chiesa di San Lorenzo** (Piazzale Papa Innocenzo IV), a stolid 14th-century Ligurian-Gothic church. It's notable for the 14th-century triptych on the altar depicting the Madonna with Child, St Catherine and St Lawrence.

❹ Bell Tower

Just opposite the church is the **bell tower**. This also served as a lookout post during the 14th century. A marble memorial above the door pays homage to the villagers who lost their lives in WWI. Stroll to the side of the tower for a partial view of the steeply terraced vineyards rising above town.

❺ Via Rollandi

Continue past the church and take the set of stairs leading up to your right. The narrow lane **Via Rollandi** takes you past village homes and one of Manarola's best restaurants (Trattoria dal Billy; p117), while offering fine views over the terraces. Continue almost to the end then take the Scalinata Pezzali back down to the main street.

❻ Manarola Harbour

Turn left and walk down to Manarola's petite **harbour**. You can zigzag your way down to the water's edge for a prime view of the Mediterranean. Although there's no beach here, a few hardy swimmers go for dips in the deep water just off the dock. Others sunbathe on the rocks fringing the shore.

❼ Punta Bonfiglio

Follow the narrow path that leads off the harbour and heads uphill. This path leads up to the hilltop lookout of **Punta Bonfiglio** (p115). From the top you'll have magnificent views over Manarola and the green hills above town. This is one of Cinque Terre's most famous panoramas; it's pure magic to be here around sunset.

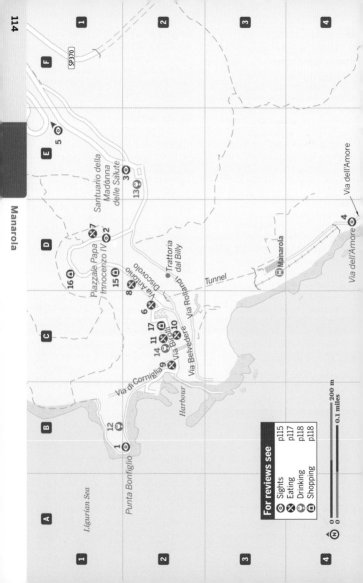

Manarola

Ligurian Sea

Punta Bonfiglio

SP370

Santuario della Madonna delle Salute

Piazzale Papa Innocenzo IV

Via di Corniglia

Via Birolli

Via Belvedere

Via Rollandi

Via Antonio Discovolo

Trattoria dal Billy

Harbour

Tunnel

Manarola

Via dell'Amore

For reviews see

⊙	Sights	p115
✕⊗	Eating	p117
⊕ ⊕	Drinking	p118
⊕	Shopping	p118

0   200 m
0   0.1 miles

⊙ N

Sights

Punta Bonfiglio

VIEWPOINT

1 ◉ MAP P114, B2

Manarola's prized viewpoint is on a rocky promontory just above the village. A rest area, including a kids playground, has been constructed here and there's also a bar just below. Nearby are the ruins of an old chapel once used as a shelter by local farmers.

Piazzale Papa Innocenzo IV

PIAZZA

2 ◉ MAP P114, D1

This small piazza is dominated by a bell tower that was once used as a defensive lookout. Opposite, the Chiesa di San Lorenzo (p113) dates from 1338 and houses a 15th-century polyptych. If you're geared up for a steep walk, from nearby Via Rollandi you can follow a path that leads through vineyards to the top of the mountain.

Reach the *piazzale* by following Via Discovolo uphill. It's about a 10-minute walk from the waterfront.

Santuario della Madonna delle Salute

WALKING

3 ◉ MAP P114, E2

The pick of all the sanctuary walks is this breathtaking traverse (trail 506) through Cinque Terre's finest vineyards to a diminutive Romanesque-meets-Gothic chapel in the tiny village of Volastra. It takes around 30 minutes. You

View of Manarola from Punta Bonfiglio

can also keep going all the way to Corniglia.

Via dell'Amore   WALKING

4 ⦿ MAP P114, D4

This beautiful coastal path that links Riomaggiore to Manarola in a leisurely 20-minute stroll was, until rockslides caused its closure in 2012, Cinque Terre's most popular. The name is a nod to the number of marriages the opening of the path engendered between villagers of the once geographically divided hamlets.

The first 200m of the path, from Manarola's train station to Bar Via dell'Amore, has reopened and it's worth the brief stroll it allows. It's uncertain when, if ever, the rest will be completed, with funding still being discussed at the time of research (much to the consternation of locals; the path is not just a scenic thoroughfare for them, but an integral part of village social life).

Cantina Cinque Terre   WINE

5 ⦿ MAP P114, E1

High above the seaside village of Manarola, Cinque Terre's largest wine producer has been cultivating vines since 1982. Over 200 grower-members make up this cooperative, which consists of dozens of lofty parcels of land, spread across the southern-facing hillsides above the crashing waves. Some of the best wines here hail from historical vineyards that date back centuries. (☏0187 92 04 35; www.cantinacinqueterre.com; SP51, Località Groppo; ⊙8am-7pm Mon-Sat, 9am-12.30pm & 2.30-7pm Sun)

Seafood spaghetti at Trattoria dal Billy

Eating

Da Aristide
SEAFOOD €€

6 ✕ MAP P114, C2

Near the tunnel leading to the train station, Aristide has tables in an old village house and in a bright, modern marque terrace on the square. Order a few of the heaped plates of stuffed anchovies or lemon-doused grilled octopus to share, or keep one of the fish ravioli or homemade pappardelle with mussels and eggplant for yourself. Reserve ahead. (☎0187 92 00 00; Via Discovolo 290; meals €25-35; ⏲8am-10pm Fri-Wed)

Cappun Magru
LIGURIAN €

7 ✕ MAP P114, D1

Located near the Chiesa di San Lorenzo, Cappun Magru is a favourite among locals for its home-style cooking, its delicious cakes and Manarola's best espressos. The seafood sandwiches made with anchovies, shrimp, salted cod and octopus are excellent, and pair well with the good DOC Cinque Terre wines. (Via Discovolo; mains €8-12; ⏲8.15am-6.30pm Tue-Sun)

Gelateria 5 Terre
GELATO €

8 ✕ MAP P114, D2

In the running for the title of Cinque Terre's best ice-cream joint. Superbly crafted flavours, including vegan and lactose-free options, never fail to delight. Don't neglect the appealing array

Trattoria da Billy

Hidden off a narrow lane in the upper reaches of town, the **Trattoria dal Billy** (Map p114, D2; ☎0187 92 06 28; www.trattoriabilly.com; Via Rollandi 122; meals €30-40) fires up some of the best seafood dishes anywhere in Cinque Terre. Start off with a mixed appetiser platter – featuring 12 different hot and cold dishes (octopus salad, lemon-drizzled anchovies, tuna with sweet onion) – then tuck into lobster pasta or swordfish with black truffle.

On clear days, book a table on the terrace for superb views. Reservations essential.

of *cannoli* (pastry shells with a sweet filling of ricotta or custard). (Via Discovolo 248; gelato from €3; ⏲11am-8pm)

Marina Piccola
SEAFOOD €€

9 ✕ MAP P114, C2

A number of fish dishes, including some tasty antipasti such as *soppressata di polpo* (sliced boiled octopus) are served up here along with right-by-the-sea views. There's a great list of Cinque Terre DOCs from both the vines above and Vernazza, as well as some excellent Vermentinos. (☎0187 92 09 23; www.hotelmarinapiccola.com; Via Birolli 120; meals €27-37; ⏲noon-10.30pm Wed-Mon; ❄🖥)

Il Porticciolo Foodrink
ITALIAN

10 MAP P114, C2

Opposite the more sedate restaurant of the same name, this lively spot with its Latin grooves serves up a small selection of inexpensive specials (pasta with swordfish, gnocchi with pesto) as well as anitpasti plates, cheese and *salumi* (charcuterie) platters and thick slices of focaccia. (Via Birolli 103; ⏰11am-10pm)

Il Porticciolo
SEAFOOD €€

11 MAP P114, C2

One of several restaurants lining the main route down to the harbour, this is a popular spot for an alfresco seafood feast. Expect seaside bustle and a fishy menu featuring classic crowd-pleasers such as spaghetti with mussels, oven-baked sea bass and crispy fried squid. (📞0187 92 00 83; Via Birolli 92; meals €30-45; ⏰11.30am-11pm)

Drinking

Nessun Dorma
BAR

12 MAP P114, B1

On a wave-kissed promontory overlooking the pastel-coloured houses of Manarola, this leafy terrace bar makes a magical setting for a sundowner. Great wine selection and plenty of creative cocktails (try a *limoncino spritz*) pair with sandwiches, salads, bruschetta and cheese platters.

This all-outdoor spot closes on rainy days. (📞340 8884133; www.nessundormacinqueterre.com; Punta Bonfiglio; ⏰noon-9.30pm)

A Piè de Campu
WINE BAR

13 MAP P114, E2

Serves up excellent wines and small plates on a terrace in the upper part of town. Come in the daytime to explore Cinque Terre's unique wines in the tasting room downstairs. Reservations recommended. Also offers guided wine tastings (p21). (📞338 2220088; apiedecampu@gmail.com; Via Discovolo; ⏰7-10pm Tue-Sun)

La Cantina dello Zio Bramante
BAR

14 MAP P114, C2

Just below street level, this friendly local watering hole is the best place in town for some late-night revelry. There's live music on weekends (and more often in the summer), good local wines on hand and you can nibble on bruschetta, sandwiches and other snacks. (Via Birolli 110; ⏰noon-midnight)

Shopping

Explora
SPORTS & OUTDOORS

15 MAP P114, D1

A small shop that stocks handy essentials for outdoor adventures, including hiking and trail-running shoes, high-performance T-shirts, hats, sunglasses, swimwear and backpacks. It also stocks good trail

Il Porticciolo

maps and a few books on Cinque Terre. You can also store luggage here, and the shop is partnered with Arbaspàa (p95), which offers tours and arranges apartment rentals in Manarola. (Via Discovolo 252; ⏰9am-7pm)

Cinque Terre Trekking
SPORTS & OUTDOORS

16 🔒 MAP P114, D1

If you're eager to get out and do some hiking but didn't bring the right gear, head uphill from the harbour to reach this outdoor outfitter. You can pick up hiking boots, trekking poles, backpacks, headlamps, moisture-wicking socks and hats, as well as T-shirts printed with those iconic red-and-white blazes so omnipresent on Cinque Terre's hiking trails. (www.cinqueterretrekking.com; Via Discovolo 108; ⏰11am-1pm & 2-7pm)

L'Emporio
ARTS & CRAFTS

17 🔒 MAP P114, C2

This colourfully decorated shop sells works by local artists and artisans: marine-life and light-house paintings done on pieces of old fishing boats, nautically themed jewellery, and tiny wooden model boats. You'll also find scarves, souvenir T-shirts (where the shop cat tends to sleep) and a few food items (pesto, olive oils, wines). (www.facebook.com/emporio.manarola; Via Birolli 82; ⏰9.30am-8.30pm)

Walking Tour 🚶

Manarola to Corniglia

On this walk, you'll climb from seaside Manarola up to the lofty village of Volastra (elevation 335m), passing through terraced vineyards and olive groves along the way. The views from up top are spectacular. Afterwards, the path continues through yet more vineyards (among the most famous in Cinque Terre) and descends through lush forest before ending in the centre of charming Corniglia.

Getting There

From Manarola train station, walk through the tunnel to the village centre, then turn right and continue up Via Discovolo to the trailhead.

❶ Manarola

Head uphill along Manarola's main street, Via Discovolo. Just around the bend take the ramp leading off to the left, with a makeshift sign indicating 'Volastra'. This scenic lane wraps back around Manarola and takes you up into the terraced vineyards above town.

❷ Stair Master

After about a 20-minute climb, you'll reach a set of stairs. You'll get a serious workout as you walk up hundreds of steps, passing fig trees, olive groves and old stone fences.

❸ Volastra

As you reach Volastra, you'll pass a shop where you can pick up cold refreshments and snacks. After about 1km, you'll reach the peaceful hamlet. Older than Manarola, Volastra was founded by the Romans in 177 BC. Settlers quickly realised the agricultural potential here; the town's name comes from 'Vicus Oleaster' – the land of the olive trees. The 12th-century village church (Nostra Signora della Salute) has a much venerated image of the Madonna. According to legend, the church bells were hidden during Saracen raids, and never recovered. It is said that the

Top Hiking Tips

The ascent is steep in places, and you'll have to keep your eyes peeled for the small faded blue arrows pointing the way while leaving Manarola. After reaching the stairs, follow the red and white blazes.

bells still toll on stormy nights. Be sure to seek out a bottle of DOC Le Coste, one of Cinque Terre's best wines. It's grown on the hills near Volastra.

❹ Pine Forest

You'll leave the village by following signs to Corniglia along trail 586. It's an exhilarating walk crossing fields and even right through someone's sea-facing backyard. As you descend, you'll enter a once cultivated area now been reclaimed by a maritime pine forest.

❺ Corniglia

The descent gets steeper as you near Corniglia. Following signs to 'Corniglia' you'll arrive at a T. Turn right and follow the lane onto Via Fieschi, Corniglia's main street. At walk's end, treat yourself to appetisers and drinks with a view at La Scuna (p108).

Explore

Riomaggiore

Cinque Terre's easternmost village, Riomaggiore is the largest of the five and acts as its unofficial HQ (the main park office is based here). Its peeling pastel buildings march down a steep ravine to a tiny harbour – the region's favourite postcard view – and glow romantically at sunset. If you are driving, the hills between here and La Spezia are spectacular to explore.

The Short List

○ **Fossola Beach (p127)** *Cooling off on the rocky beach just outside of the village.*

○ **Santuario della Madonna di Montenero (p127)** *Making the ascent up to this hillside sanctuary for fabulous views over the coast.*

○ **A Pié de Mà (p129)** *Enjoying a sundowner at this open-air spot set perfectly above the crashing waves.*

○ **Rio Bistrot (p127)** *Feasting on mouthwatering seafood while overlooking Riomaggiore's marina.*

○ **Enoteca d'uu Scintu (p129)** *Picking up bottles of limoncino, top-notch pesto and other gifts at this small, well-stocked shop.*

Getting There & Around

🚆 Riomaggiore is on the main train line for the Trenitalia Cinque Terre Express trains and is only seven to 10 minutes from La Spezia.

Riomaggiore Map on p126

Riomaggiore harbour AFRIANDI / GETTY IMAGES ©

Walking Tour 🥾

Riomaggiore

On this looping stroll around Cinque Terre's largest village, you'll enjoy marvellous views over the seaside and visit iconic buildings, including a 14th-century church. You'll also get a glimpse of Riomaggiore's murals, which depict the back-breaking work of Cinque Terre farmers. The stroll ends by the seaside at Riomaggiore's somewhat concealed rocky beach.

Walk Facts

Start Riomaggiore train station; 🚆 Riomaggiore

End Fossola Beach; 🚆 Riomaggiore

Length 4km; one to two hours

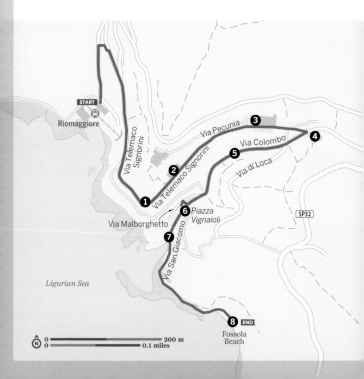

❶ Viewpoint

Starting off from the train station, walk uphill, take the first stairs to your right, and continue ascending until you reach a **viewpoint** overlooking the village. Here locals gather on park benches against a mesmerising backdrop.

❷ Murals

As the path winds around, you'll pass by **murals** of grape pickers and fishers above a busty sea goddess adorning Riomaggiore's city hall. These works were painted by the Argentine-Italian artist Silvio Benedetto (born 1938).

❸ Chiesa di San Giovanni Battista

The heart of spiritual life in the village, Chiesa di **San Giovanni Battista** (p127) occupies a strategic perch watching over the town. The 14th-century church is devoted to the town's patron saint, John the Baptist, whose feast day is celebrated with fervour on 24 June.

❹ Oratorio di Santa Maria Assunta

A few streets up, you'll see the **Oratorio di Santa Maria Assunta** (Via Colombo; ⏲9am-8pm). This small chapel is notable for the 14th-century wooden statue of the *Madonna delle catene* (Madonna of the chains), a reminder of the enslavement suffered by town inhabitants following raids by pirates in the Middle Ages.

❺ Via Colombo

Leaving the oratory, walk downhill. **Via Colombo** is packed with shops and cafes, with outdoor dining spots offering excellent vantage points of the passing people parade.

❻ Piazza Vignaioli

At Via Colombo's end, climb the stairs to the sunny **Piazza Vignaioli**, which is another key communal spot in Riomaggiore. More Benedetto murals of grape harvesters and labourers front one side of the square.

❼ Marina

Head back down the stairs, and descend another set of stairs to head down to the **marina**. Riomaggiore's tiny waterfront plaza has just a couple of restaurants, and is sometimes full of boats. During bad weather, locals haul their watercraft out of the sea and onto the sloping square.

❽ Fossola Beach

Take the ramp leading up to the left and follow this around for Instagram-worthy views of the seaside. The path leads past the ferry boat dock and sunbathers, and eventually winds around to Riomaggiore's small rocky **Fossola Beach** (p127) – the perfect spot for a refreshing dip on hot summer days.

Riomaggiore

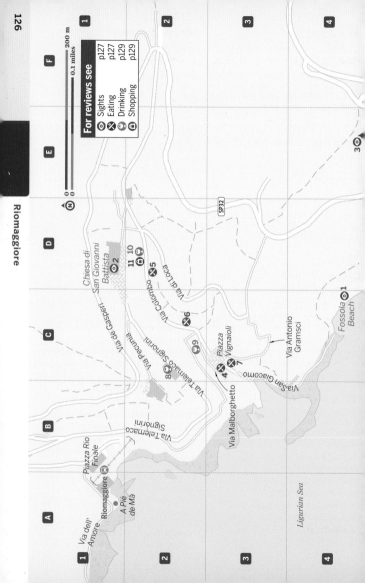

200 m
0.1 miles

For reviews see
- ⊙ Sights — p127
- ✕ Eating — p127
- 🍷 Drinking — p129
- 🛍 Shopping — p129

Via dell' Amore

Piazza Rio Finale

Riomaggiore

A Piè de Mà

Via de Gasperi

Chiesa di San Giovanni Battista

Via Telemaco Signorini

Via Pecunia

Via Colombo

Via di Loca

SP32

Piazza Vignaioli

Via Malborghetto

Via Antonio Gramsci

Via San Giacomo

Fossola ⊙1 Beach

Ligurian Sea

Sights

Fossola Beach BEACH

1 MAP P126, C4

This small pebbly beach is situated immediately southeast of the Riomaggiore marina. Take the short trail that leads just past the harbour to get here. The shore is rugged and delightfully secluded from the village (though it gets packed with holidaymakers during the summer months); it is also remarkably photogenic with the Ligurian sea waters framed by the steep hillsides. Swimmers should be wary of the dangerous strong currents here.

Chiesa di San Giovanni Battista CHURCH

2 MAP P126, D1

Set in the upper part of town, this striking church was founded in 1340 but received a facelift in 1870 giving it a neo-Gothic facade. Original 14th-century elements, however, remain, including the rose window made of Carrara marble and the side entrances that are decorated with zoomorphic and anthropomorphic images.

Inside the church contains a wooden crucifix carved by Anton Maria Maragliano and a triptych depicting the Madonna and Child with Sts Rocco and Sebastiano that dates from the 15th century. (Via Pecunia)

Riomaggiore to Santuario della Madonna di Montenero WALKING

3 MAP P126, E4

Trail 593V ascends for around an hour from Riomaggiore, up steps and past walled gardens to a restored 18th-century chapel with a frescoed ceiling, which sits atop an astounding lookout high above the coastline.

Find the trailhead down by the waterfront. An alternative route up to the sanctuary, SVA (formerly No 3) starts at the top of Riomaggiore; take Via Colombo uphill and look for the signs.

Eating

Rio Bistrot LIGURIAN €€

4 MAP P126, C3

One of Riomaggiore's top dining destinations, Rio Bistrot earns rave reviews for its beautifully prepared seafood dishes – with selections changing daily depending on the local catch. The prices are quite high, but the service, elegant setting and lovely waterfront views are all top-notch. Be sure to book an outdoor table when the skies are clear. (☑0187 92 06 16; Via San Giacomo 10; meals €40-55; ☉noon-3pm & 7-10pm)

La Cantina del Macellaio STEAK €€

5 MAP P126, D2

A surprising find in seafood-centric Cinque Terre, La Cantina del Macellaio fires up melt-in-your-mouth braised beef, pasta with wild boar and a few other simple but beautifully executed dishes. The incredibly accommodating staff and good wines on hand make for a memorable night out. (☎0187 92 07 88; www.facebook.com/lacantinadelmacellaio.rio; Via Colombo 103; meals €35-45; ⏲noon-3pm & 7-11pm)

Il Pescato Cucinato
SEAFOOD €

 6 🍴 MAP P126, C2

Riomaggiore's standout street food is a mound of fresh fried seafood – calamari, anchovies, shrimp, cod – stuffed into a paper cone and served on the go. Vegetarians can opt for chips (fries) or

fried veggies. Take your seafood treat down to the waterfront for munching to million-dollar views. (Via Colombo 199; snacks around €6; ⏲11.30am-11pm)

Dau Cila
SEAFOOD €€

 7 🍴 MAP P126, C3

Perched within pebble-lobbing distance of Riomaggiore's wee harbour, Dau Cila is a smart, kitsch-free zone, and specialises in classic seafood and hyper-local wines. Pair the best Cinque Terre whites with cold plates such as smoked tuna with apples and lemon, or lemon-marinated anchovies. (☎0187 76 00 32; www.ristorantedaucila.com; Via San Giacomo 65; meals €40-45; ⏲12.30-3pm & 7-10.30pm)

Enoteca d'uu Scintu

Drinking

Fuori Rotta WINE BAR

8 🚇 MAP P126, C2

Set on a hillside lane, the friendly Fuori Rotta makes a fine escape from the busier spots by the harbour. Here you can sit at outdoor tables overlooking the rooftops of Riomaggiore while enjoying refreshing *spritzes* and tasty snacks and sharing platters (full meals also available). In the morning, this is an unbeatable spot for a cappuccino and a pastry. (📞0187 92 08 38; www.facebook.com/Fuori rottario; Via Telemaco Signorini 48; ⏰9.30am-8.30pm Thu-Tue)

Bar O'Netto BAR

9 🚇 MAP P126, C2

Riomaggiore's liveliest drinking den is a local institution – around in one form or another since 1921. Stop in here to catch up on village gossip (if you speak Italian), and enjoy frothy pints (microbrews available), inexpensive wines and plenty of good cheer. In January and February, it's about the only place in town that stays open. (Via Malborghetto 4; ⏰7am-1am)

Vertical Bar BAR

10 🚇 MAP P126, D2

With outdoor tables on a prime stretch of Via Colombo, Vertical Bar is a great spot for coffee or cocktails – depending on which direction you're steering your day. You won't find better versions of classic drinks like the Moscow Mule, and the young owner Fiorenzo makes everyone feel right at home. (Via Colombo 76; ⏰9am-11pm)

Sundowners at A Pié de Mà

A delightful spot for an afternoon pick-me-up, this open-air **gem** (Map p126, A1; 📞0187 92 10 37; www.facebook.com/apiede mariomaggiore; Via dell'Amore 55; ⏰11am-6.30pm Wed-Mon Oct-May, to 11pm Jun-Sep) has a terrace perched right over Riomaggiore's wave-kissed shoreline. You'll find local craft beers (including La Spezia's Birrificio del Golfo on draught) as well as coffees, a few desserts and a fine selection of both red and white wines from Cinque Terre.

To get here, follow signs to the Via dell'Amore trail, to the left as you leave the station.

Shopping

Enoteca d'uu Scintu FOOD

11 🔒 MAP P126, D2

You'll find a wide range of local products at this shop near the top of Via Colombo. This is the place for Genoese pesto, extra virgin olive oils, lemon-scented soaps, pretty bottles of *limoncino* (locally made lemon liqueur), grappa and wines, plus sweet treats (handsomely wrapped amaretto biscuits). (📞0187 92 09 65; Via Colombo 84; ⏰9am-10pm)

Top Experience 📷

Sentiero Rosso – Alta Via delle Cinque Terre

Just a few kilometres shy of a marathon, the 38km Alta Via delle Cinque Terre – which runs from Porto Venere to Levanto – dangles a tempting challenge to experienced walkers who aim to complete it in one or two days. For every 100 people you see on the Sentiero Azzurro, there are only one or two up here plying their way along this difficult but highly rewarding route.

Getting There

Set out early and catch the train to La Spezia, and from there a bus onward to Porto Venere.

❶ Porto Venere

Once you arrive in Porto Venere, find your way to the Piazza Giacamo Bastreri and take the stairs leading up to the Castello Doria (pictured). You'll soon see the first of many signs, indicating you're on the right path, with Campiglia the next stop from here.

❷ Forte Muzzerone

You'll follow along the castle walls as you ascend, eventually emerging onto a narrow rocky path that skirts the coast. You'll pass the ruins of Forte Muzzerone, a 19th-century fortification used in both world wars. Nearby cliff faces are a favourite spot for rock climbers.

❸ Marmo Portoro

As you leave the fort behind, you'll pass a quarry of *marmo portoro* (portoro marble). The stone found here is a valuable black marble with goldish-yellow streaks. Marble extraction near Porto Venere dates back to the Roman era, and in the 1860s there were 30 active quarries throughout the region. Today, however, this is the only quarry still in operation.

❹ Pitone

The climb gets steep and crosses some sheer drop-offs in places. Eventually you'll reach one of the most striking lookouts over Porto Venere. Known as Pitone, this ledge juts out above the hilltop, providing a natural balcony high above the sea. Here you can look back to the craggy peaks you've just passed, and see the islands of Palmaria, and Tino, and a tiny bit of Tinetto, just offshore from Porto Venere.

❺ Campiglia

The ascent continues, at times crossing over boulders and jagged rocks, and through dense Mediterranean vegetation. It's another

★ Top Tips

● If you plan on doing the whole hike, one of the best places to start is at Porto Venere (p136).

● Preparation: wear good walking shoes, a hat and sun protection, and make sure you have adequate water (there are limited places to get water on the trail).

✕ Take a Break

The best place to stop for a bite on the trail is at the **Colle del Telegrafo** (☏0187 76 05 61; Località Colle del Telegrafo; meals €25-35; ⏱9am-8pm Tue-Sun), which has delicious snacks (and anchovies), plus fabulous views.

After an epic walk, treat yourself to a celebratory drink at Contro Vento (p63) in Levanto.

Top Experience Sentiero Rosso – Alta Via delle Cinque Terre

40 minutes or so of climbing to reach the small village of Campiglia (roughly 6km from Porto Venere). You'll pass the ruins of a 17th-century windmill just before reaching the town. You'll walk right past the village church (on your left) as you cross through Campiglia. Follow the AV5T signs and continue straight through town.

❻ Valico di Sant'Antonio

Up is the only way to go as you keep climbing past orchards and vineyards. You'll have views over La Spezia bay and will get some cool relief as you enter a forest of pine, chestnut and oak trees. Around 2.3km from Campiglia you'll reach the Valico di Sant'Antonio (St Anthony Pass; elevation 508m). There's a small chapel, and a fountain where you can get cold water;

you might also see a few folks exercising in the Palestra nel Verde (open-air gym) set in the surrounding woods.

❼ Colle del Telegrafo

It's a fairly flat stretch up to Colle del Telegrafo (Telegraph Hill), so named for the telegraph wires that used to be strung here. The 4km walk from Campiglia takes you about one hour. You'll know you've arrived when you reach the restaurant named after the spot. You can refuel with plates of bruschetta and cold drinks, while relaxing on the terrace overlooking the sea.

❽ Cigoletta

If you're ready to call it a day, you can take trail 593 (SVA3) down to Riomaggiore – though it's worth

plugging on as the worst of the climbing is behind you. Continue toward Cigoletta (elevation 611m), another 7km or so – around three hours walking. You'll go from open, scrubby terrain to dense forest, with the Mediterranean just a blue suggestion through the thick foliage.

❾ Il Termine

Il Termine is an open clearing roughly 7km from Cigoletta. There are some gentle uphill climbs on this stretch as you pass along the slopes of Mt Malpertuso, the highest point of Cinque Terre at 815m. The sea will seem very far away, though you'll have some nice views in the opposite direction of the lush valleys in the interior. Sometimes covered in mists, this is an enchanting, little-visited stretch of Cinque Terre that feels a world removed from the bustle in the villages far below.

At Il Termine, you'll reach a T-intersection where SP51 intersects with the busier SP38. Cross SP38 and walk towards the left about 50m (follow the brown sign for Santuario di Saviore). Then look for the faint somewhat overgrown path leading off the highway up to the right. If instead, you want to visit the Madonna di Saviore and continue down to Monterosso, you'll have to walk along the highway to rejoin the trail 1km further along.

❿ Colle di Gritta

It's just under 2km from Il Termine to Crocettola, a pass located beneath Mt Crocettola (elevation 609m). From here the AV5T turns into the paved road that continues far north to Bardellone, well beyond the boundaries of the national park. Instead, you'll turn left (southwestward) here, and follow the 591c downhill to Colle di Gritta.

⓫ Punta Mesco

At Col de Gritta you'll continue in the same direction along track 591. For the full experience, go all the way to Sant'Antonio on the Punta Mesco, a distance of just over 4km. However, if energy is in short supply, you can shave off a few kilometres by taking trails 572 or 573 to Levanto. Those who make the trek to Sant'Antonio (a 75-minute hike from Colle di Gritta) will be rewarded with spectacular views over a vast stretch of Mediterranean coastline. There's also the ruins of a 14th-century church and hermitage.

⓬ Levanto

From here, the journey follows the coastline northwest to Levanto, about 4km from Sant'Antonio. You'll have fine views throughout the walk, passing through pines, Mediterranean scrub and forests of holm oaks. At long last, you'll see the rooftops of Levanto, and descend into the centre of town.

Explore ⊘
La Spezia &
the Bay of Poets

The bustling but underrated city of La Spezia makes for a nicely urban, if supremely easygoing, base. It fronts a picturesque bay named after the English poets who fell for the region in the 1820s. With mountains looming on the horizon and cliffs plummeting into the sea, there's an unrivalled beauty to the former fishing villages of Porto Venere, Lerici and Tellaro around the bay.

The Short List

○ *Grotta di Byron (p137)* Watching the gulls soar above this breathtaking terrace named after one of Porto Venere's great English admirers.

○ *Palmaria (p145)* Hiking around the island of Palmaria, enjoying dramatic views at every turn.

○ *Tellaro (p140)* Visiting ruins above the village, followed by afternoon drinks on a seaside piazza.

○ *Castello di Lerici (p139)* Taking in the view over the dramatic Golfo dei Poeti from this cliffside castle above Lerici.

○ *Resilience Cafe (p145)* Joining locals over cocktails at this creative drinking den in La Spezia.

Getting There & Around

🚃 La Spezia has frequent rail links to the Cinque Terre villages as well as to Genoa.

⛴ The Cinque Terre villages and other coastal towns are easily accessible by train and boat.

🚌 From Via Fiume below La Spezia's train station, buses 11 and P run to Porto Venere (€2.50); buses L and S go to Lerici.

La Spezia Map on p142

Grotta di Byron and Castello Doria (p137), Porto Venere
BUMIHILLS / SHUTTERSTOCK ©

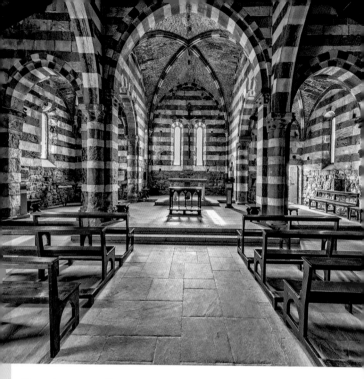

Top Sight 📷
Porto Venere

Perched on the dreamy Golfo dei Poeti's western promontory, the historic fishing port's sinuous seven- and eight-storey harbourfront houses form an almost impregnable citadel around the muscular Castello Doria. The town remains a romantic, scenic place for a day trip, or a relaxing base for exploring the coast.

Tourist Office

www.prolocoportovenere.it

Piazza Bastreri 7

🕐 10am-noon & 3-7pm Jun-Aug, to 6pm Thu-Tue Sep-May

Grotta di Byron

At the end of the quay, a Cinque Terre panorama unfolds from the rocky terraces of a cave formerly known as Grotta Arpaia. Lord Byron once swam across the gulf from here to Lerici to visit the resident Shelleys. Despite the cave's collapse, the rocky terraces remain quite beautiful and suitably dishevelled and affecting.

To add to the frisson, know that traces of a pagan temple dedicated to Venus (hence a suggestion to the name 'Venere') have been uncovered here, as well as inside the black-and-white-marble **Chiesa di San Pietro** (pictured; www.parrocchiaportovenere.it; ☺8.30am-7pm Jun-Sep, to 5.30pm Oct-May). Just off the promontory, you can see the tiny islands of Palmaria, Tino and Tinetto.

Castello Doria

No one knows when the original **castle** (adult/reduced €5/3; ☺10am-6pm Apr-Oct) was built, though the current structure – a formidable example of Genoese military architecture – dates from the 16th century. Aside from admiring the fine construction, there isn't much to see inside, but views from the terraced gardens are magnificent.

History

The Romans built Portus Veneris as a base en route from Gaul to Spain, and in later years the Byzantines, Lombards, Genoese and Napoleon all passed through here and made the most of its spectacular natural defences. Its appeal is, however, not just strategic, its beauty drawing the poet Byron who famously swam from the now collapsed Grotta Arpaia's rocky cove to San Terenzo to visit fellow poet Percy Shelley (it was to be renamed Grotta di Byron for him).

★ **Getting There & Away**

Hourly buses run to Porto Venere (€2.50) from Via Fiume, below La Spezia train station.

From late March to October, Consorzio Marittimo Turistico Cinque Terre Golfo dei Poeti sails from Porto Venere to/from Cinque Terre villages (all day, all stops €35, one way €27, afternoon-only ticket €27).

Note that you can't park in the town during summer; a parking area is located just outside the town and a shuttle service (€1 per person) operates all day.

✕ **Take a Break**

Grab some anchovy-stuffed *panini* from **Anciua** (☎331 7719605; Via Cappellini 40; snacks from €6; ☺11am-7pm), or pick up a whole spinach pie for a picnic on the waterfront.

Top Sight 📷
Lerici & San Terenzo

Magnolia, yew and cedar trees grow in the 1930s public gardens at Lerici, an exclusive retreat of terraced villas clinging to the cliffs along its beach, and in another age Byron and Shelley sought inspiration here. From Lerici, a scenic 3km coastal stroll leads northwest to San Terenzo, a seaside village with a sandy beach and Genoese castle.

Tourist Information

There are several tourist information kiosks in the area, including on the Lerici waterfront near Piazza Garibaldi.

Castello di Lerici

On a promontory high above the shoreline, Lerici's **castle** (pictured; Piazzetta San Giorgio; admission free; ⏰10am–noon & 3-6pm Tue-Sun May, Jun & mid-Sep–Oct, 10am–noon & 6-11pm daily Jul–mid-Sep) has played a pivotal role protecting the city since the Middle Ages. Rebuilt various times over the years, the citadel today hosts changing exhibitions spread among various stone-walled chambers. There are also fabulous views from its lofty terraces.

Via Cavour

Just off Piazza Garibaldi in Lerici, this atmospheric pedestrian lane is sprinkled with colourful boutiques, a focacceria and wine shop, and some appealing seafood-focused restaurants. Anchoring the western end of the street is the St Roch Oratory and tower, built in the early 16th century.

Beaches

San Terenzo has an appealing sandy beach with free sections as well as places to hire loungers and umbrellas. A long breakwall 100m offshore ensures particularly calm waters here.

For something more isolated, check out the wild, cliff-backed beaches hidden behind the Castello di Lerici. Reach the first beach by heading through the tunnel (under the castle) that leads off Via Giuseppe Mazzini and taking the stairs down to the water. To reach the other beaches, you'll have to clamber over the rocks (wear good shoes) – not advised if you have children in tow.

★ **Getting There & Around**

ATC Esercizio (www.atcesercizio.it) buses run to Lerici and San Terenzo from La Spezia's train station, a 35-minute trip (€2.50).

Parking is quite limited in the area. You're better off getting around on foot within the villages and by bus when travelling between Lerici or San Terenzo and Tellaro.

✕ **Take a Break**

Just across from Piazza Garibaldi in Lerici, **Dal Pudu** (Piazza Garibaldi 10; mains €10-18; ⏰noon-3pm & 7-10pm) is a takeaway spot serving some of the best seafood in town. Go early to score a table out front.

Top Sight 📷
Tellaro

Backed by lush hillsides covered in olive trees and oaks, the faded pink and orange houses of Tellaro overlook several small bays on a ruggedly beautiful stretch of the Italian Riviera coastline. Just a few narrow lanes wind through the tightly compact village, past hidden squares and scenic overlooks before reaching the rocky shore.

Tourist Information

Punto Informativo

📞 0187 96 91 64

Via Fiascherino

🕐 9am-1pm Tue-Sun mid-Jun–mid-Sep, 9am-1pm Sat & Sun only Apr–mid-Jun & mid-Sep–Oct

Scenic Walks

There are numerous walking trails in the area. You can plan a route between Lerici and Tellaro, strolling up along the hillsides overlooking old olive groves, passing abandoned villages and catching some fabulous views over the coastline.

On a walking track just above Tellaro stands the ruins of Portesone, a former rural village that was abandoned in the 1600s (allegedly owing to a plague epidemic). You can see the falling-down stone buildings, slowly being reclaimed by the forest, with olive trees, figs and poppies growing wild in the roofless interiors.

Portesone is about a 15-minute uphill climb from Lerici. Take trail 431 up from the main road (Via Fiascherino/SP26), located just north of the big church Stella Maris. Once you reach Portesone, you can keep going north to Barbazzano – another abandoned village – via trail 433.

Chiesa di San Giorgio

Built in the second half of the 16th century, the imposing Chiesa di San Giorgio occupies a strategic point overlooking the seaside. Over the portal, a bas relief in Carrara marble depicts a horse-riding St George trampling a dragon. Looming above are the three bells of the church tower, which were allegedly rung by an octopus to warn against a Saracen attack in the 1660s.

Nearby Beaches

Although there's no beach in Tellaro, nearby **Fiascherino** (a little over 1km north) has splendid sandy beaches, set on two sheltered bays that are ideal for swimming. It's hard not to fall for this area, as English writer DH Lawrence did while living here in 1913.

★ **Getting There & Away**

Buses run every hour or so from Lerici's Piazza Garibaldi to Tellaro (€1.50), passing Fiascherino along the way.

✕ **Take a Break**

Osteria del Borgo (☎0187 96 68 68; Via Gramsci 22; meals €35-45; ⏰noon-2.30pm & 7-10pm) is the best choice for seafood serving up mouthwatering plates of fresh fish, seafood pastas and various octopus dishes. Reserve ahead or go early to score a table on the terrace overlooking the waterfront.

Bar la Marina (Piazza Quattro Novembre 2; ⏰10am-10pm) dispenses spritzes and wine to tables on the tiny port's cobblestones. Time your visit for sunset and you'll understand what so enchanted Byron and Shelley.

A **B** **C** **D**

1

Train Station

Colle di
La Spezia

0 _____ 200 m
0 _____ 0.1 miles

Via Paleocapa

Via Fiume

Piazza
Saint Bon

2

Piazza
Garibaldi

Via del
Prione

4

9

Corso Cavour

Via del Prione

3

Museo
Amedeo Lia

Via XX Settembre

Via Garibaldi

Viale Garibaldi

3

Via XXVII Marzo

Via XX Settembre

1

Castello di
San Giorgio

Piazza di
Giuseppe
Verdi

Piazza
Cavour

Via Gramsci

Via Colombo

Via Fratelli Rosselli

6

Viale Amendola

Via Urbano Rattazzi

5

7

Via Felice Cavallotti

Via Fazio

8

Via Domenico Chiodo

Via Giovanni Minzoni

Piazza
Cesare
Battisti

10

Parco
S Allende

Viale Giuseppe Mazzini

4

Canale Lagora

Via Sapri

Corso Cavour

Piazza
Domenico
Chiodo

Viale Armando
Diaz

Viale Italia

Passeggiata
Constantino Morin

5

Naval
Port

Naval
Base

Museo Tecnico Navale
della Spezia

2

Via Carlo
Bertella

6

For reviews see	
Sights	p143
Eating	p144
Drinking	p145

A **B** **C** **D**

Sights

Castello di San Giorgio   CASTLE

1 ⊙ MAP P142, C3

An assortment of local archaeo-logical artefacts from prehistoric to medieval times are displayed at the city's hilltop fortifications. You'll see finely crafted statues, exquisite mosaics, ceramics, jewellery and even some remark-ably intact glassware. There are fabulous views over the city and waterfront from the terraces. The castle itself is an imposing work dating from the 14th century, though it has undergone various redesigns over the years. (http://museodelcastello.spezianet.it; Via XXVII Marzo; adult/reduced €5.50/4; ⊙9.30am-12.30pm Mon, 9.30am-12.30pm & 2-5pm Wed-Sun, from 10.30am Jun-Aug)

Museo Tecnico Navale della Spezia   MUSEUM

2 ⊙ MAP P142, C5

Maritime lovers shouldn't miss the world's oldest naval museum, which is reached via a narrow bridge a few blocks southwest of Parco Salvador Allende. The halls contain all manner of naval curiosities, including small models of sailing vessels from around the globe, otherworldly diving suits and a special area dedicated to Marconi's wireless invention. Upstairs, the Sala delle Polene is a hauntingly beautiful room with 28 figureheads that once adorned large sailing ships. The oldest, a sword- and shield-wielding Minerva, dates from 1738. (☏0187 78 47 63; Viale Amendola 1; €1.55; ⊙8.30am-7.30pm)

Museo Amedeo Lia   MUSEUM

3 ⊙ MAP P142, B3

This fine-arts museum in a restored 17th-century friary is La Spezia's star cultural attrac-tion. The collection spans from the 13th to 18th centuries and includes paintings by masters such as Tintoretto, Montagna, Titian and Pietro Lorenzetti. Also on show are Roman bronzes and ecclesiastical treasures, such as Limoges crucifixes and illuminat-ed musical manuscripts. (http://museolia.spezianet.it; Via del Prione 234; adult/reduced €10/7; ⊙10am-6pm Tue-Sun)

Via del Prione   STREET

4 ⊙ MAP P142, B3

If you have limited time in La Spezia, make sure you prioritise a stroll along this picturesque pedestrian lane that winds through the historic centre. This is one of the oldest streets in town and is sprinkled with shops, cafes, restaurants and several museums (plus the tourist office). If you keep going, you'll reach the public gardens and the waterfront just beyond.

Eating

Il Papeoto   VEGETARIAN €€

5 MAP P142, B4

This friendly *osteria* (casual tavern) turns out Instagram-worthy plates of creative, cruelty-free delicacies. Rich, complex flavours feature prominently in dishes like gnocchi with salty ricotta cheese and almonds or crispy egg asparagus with saffron sauce; don't overlook the imaginative desserts. The setting inspires zen-like calm, with vintage botanical prints on the walls, chic industrial fixtures, and touches of greenery. Reservations recommended. (☏0187 150 95 68; www.facebook.com/ristorantevegetariano; Via Urbano Rattazzi 25; meals €26-32; ⏱7.30-10.30pm Mon-Sat; ✍)

Osteria all'Inferno dal 1905   LIGURIAN €

6 MAP P142, B4

Go early to score a table at this sprawling subterranean *osteria*, a famed destination for *la cucina spezzina* (La Spezia cooking). True to its name, this restaurant has been around since 1905, garnering five generations of fans for its hearty plates of codfish stew, fried anchovies, wild boar with polenta and other satisfying comfort fare. (☏0187 2 94 58; Via Lorenzo Costa 3; meals €20-30; ⏱12.15-2.30pm & 7.30-10.30pm Mon-Sat; ✍)

Museo Tecnico Navale della Spezia (p143)

La Pia Centenaria

LIGURIAN €

7 MAP P142, C4

Founded in 1887, La Pia is a much-loved icon in La Spezia. Piping-hot slices of *farinata* (chickpea-flour flatbread) is the big draw, though there's also perfectly cooked slabs of pizzas, satisfying focaccia (including the cheese-packed *focaccia di Recco*) and quiche-like vegetable tort. The dining room is a casual affair, though there's also a takeaway window next door. (www.lapia.it; Via Magenta 12; farinata/pizza from €2/4; ⏰10am-10pm)

Drinking

Resilience Cafe

BAR

8 MAP P142, D4

An atmospheric spot for a pre- or post-dinner drink, the Resilience Cafe exudes effortless style, with its wine-red walls, shelves of books, twinkling chandeliers and vintage furniture. The well-made cocktails are served in fine glassware and you can design your own bruschetta, and cheese and meat boards. (www.facebook.com/resiliencecafe; Via Vanicella 8; ⏰6pm-midnight Mon-Thu, to 1am Fri & Sat)

La Taverna del Metallo

BAR

9 MAP P142, B3

That heart-warming combination of heavy metal and medieval ambience draws young revellers to this drinking den off Via del Prione. Tapered candles, stone walls and low-playing Megadeth set just the right mood for indulging in some outstanding beers from Italy, Belgium, Germany and Ireland. There's a full menu, too. (☎349 8639139; www.facebook.com/latavernadelmetallo; Via Cernaia 17; ⏰8pm-2am)

Odioilvino

WINE BAR

10 MAP P142, C4

A dark, bohemian, elegantly dishevelled wine bar on a pretty street in the pedestrian centre, Odioilvino is a fine place to relax with locals over a Ligurian wine or a local craft beer. Small plates such as a fish tartare, anchovies with pesto, cheese plates, or octopus salad are on offer, too. (☎392 2141825; www.facebook.com/Odioilvino; Via Daniele Manin 11; ⏰12.30-3.30pm & 6-11pm Mon-Thu, to midnight Fri & Sat)

Survival Guide

Cattedrale di San Lorenzo, Genoa (p42) OLENA Z / SHUTTERSTOCK ©

Before You Go

Book Your Stay

o Reserve high season months in advance.

o In Cinque Terre, many locals rent out rooms, some with terraces. Look for *affittacamere* signs, and ask at restaurants bars and shops.

o La Spezia and Levanto are fine bases for exploring Cinque Terre, with good train access.

Useful Websites

B&B Italia (www.bb italia.it) Small selection of affordable B&Bs in Liguria.

Secret Places (www. secretplaces.com) Track down little-known gems.

Best Budget

La Superba (www.la-superba.com) Lovingly cared-for place on the two top floors of an old *palazzo* in Genoa.

L'Eremo sul Mare (www.eremosulmare. com) Charming cliff-side villa near Vernazza.

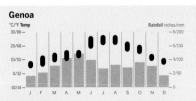

When to Go

o **Spring** March to May can be wet, though you can often beat the crowds and score low-season discounts on lodging.

o **Summer** Crowds pack Cinque Terre from June to early September; but it's a good time for beach-going, hiking and other outdoor activities.

o **Autumn** Late September and October can be an excellent time to visit, with pleasant weather and fewer crowds.

o **Winter** Many hotels, restaurants and shops close for the season. Rainy weather makes for treacherous hiking, and some walking trails close.

Il Magan (www.vernaz zani5terre.it) Four appealingly simple, rustic rooms in Corniglia, all with spectacular views.

Alta Marea (www.affit tacamerealtamarea.it) In La Spezia, this attractive B&B has airy and bright rooms.

Best Midrange

Palazzo Grillo (www. hotelpalazzogrillo.it) *Palazzo* in Genoa with original frescoes and stylish contemporary flourishes.

Hotel Marina Piccola (www.hotelmarina piccola.com) Big, comfortable, contemporary rooms, some with seaview, in Manarola.

Arbaspàa (www.arba spaa.com) Manarola-based outfit that rents out beautiful apartments in all the Cinque Terre villages.

La Mala (www.lamala .it) Contemporary rooms with fabulous sea views in the heights above Vernazza.

Best Top End

La Torretta Lodge
(www.torrettas.com)
Boutique hotel in Manarola with antiques and murals.

Blu di Te (www.bludite.com) Beautiful villa in Santa Margherita Ligure.

Villa Rosmarino (www.villarosmarino.com)
Handsome 20th-century furniture and contemporary artworks in Camogli.

Grand Hotel Villa Balbi (www.villabalbi.it) A lavish 17th-century villa in Sestri Levante.

Arriving in Genoa & Cinque Terre

Cristoforo Colombo Airport

Regular domestic and international services, including Ryanair flights to London Stansted, use **Cristoforo Colombo Airport** (📞010 6 01 51; www.airport.genova.it), 6km west of Genoa.

Genoa Train Stations

Genoa's Stazione Principe and Stazione Brignole are linked by very frequent trains to Milan (€13.50 to €22, 1½ to two hours), Pisa (€27, two hours), Rome (€64, five hours) and Turin (€12.40, two hours).

La Spezia Central Train Station

La Spezia is on the Genoa–Rome railway line and is also connected to Milan (€29, 3½ hours, every two hours), Turin (€40 to €42, 3½ hours, several daily) and Pisa (€8 to €16, 50 to 80 minutes, almost hourly).

Getting Around

Train

◦ Frequent trains connect Genoa with Camogli, Santa Margherita Ligure, Rapallo, Sestri Levante, Levanto, the five villages of Cinque Terre and La Spezia.

Ferry

◦ Ferries connect many coastal destinations here, with boats typically running from April to October.

◦ From Genoa's Porto Antico, **Golfo Paradiso SNC** (www.golfoparadiso.it) goes to Camogli (one way/return €10/17), Portofino (€15/24) and Cinque Terre (€21/38). **Consorzio Liguria Via Mare** (www.liguriaviamare.it) runs seasonal trips to Camogli, San Fruttuoso and Portofino; Monterosso in Cinque Terre; and Porto Venere.

Bus

Portofino Bus 82 runs to Portofino from outside the waterfront tourist office in Santa Margherita Ligure (€1.80, every 15 to 30 minutes).

Porto Venere From La Spezia hourly buses (11 or P) go from Via Fiume just below the train station to Porto Venere (€2.50, 30 minutes).

Lerici and San Terenzo Buses depart every 30 to 60 minutes from La Spezia's train station (€2.50, around 35 minutes).

Car & Motorcycle

Private vehicles are not allowed beyond village entrances and during high-volume days roads between villages can be closed. If you're arriving by car or motorcycle, you'll need to pay to park in designated car parks though these are often full. In some villages, minibus shuttles depart from the car parks.

Essential Information

Accessible Travel

o Cobblestone streets and steep hills make getting around difficult for wheelchair users, and most buildings lack lifts.

o Visit Tren Italia (www.rfi.it/rfi-en/For-persons-with-disability) for details on barrier-free train stations.

Business Hours

Banks 8.30am to 1.30pm and 2.45pm to 4.30pm Monday to Friday

Bars & cafes 7.30am to 8pm, sometimes to 1am

Restaurants noon to 3pm and 7.30pm to 10pm

Shops 9am to 1pm and 3.30pm to 7.30pm Monday to Saturday

Discount Cards

o The **Card Musei** (24/48 hours €12/20) gives free admission to over 20 of Genoa's museums.

o The **Cinque Terre card** (p90) gives unlimited use of walking paths and electric village buses. A one-/two-day card costs €7.50/14.50. For unlimited train trips between Cinque Terre towns, the card costs €16/29.

Electricity

Type C
220V/50Hz

Type F
230V/50Hz

Emergencies

Genoa Police (☎ 010 5 36 61; Via Armando Diaz 2)

LGBT+ Travellers

Gay.it (www.gay.it) Website featuring LGBT+ news, features and gossip.

Pride (www.prideon line.it) Culture, politics, travel and health with an LGBT+ focus.

Money

o ATMs (*bancomat*) are widely available.

o Virtually all midrange and top-end hotels accept credit cards, as do most restaurants and large shops.

Public Holidays

Capodanno 1 January

Epifania 6 January

Pasquetta (Easter Monday) March/April

Giorno della Liberazione 25 April

Festa del Lavoro 1 May

Festa della Repubblica 2 June

Ferragosto 15 August

Festa di Ognisanti 1 November

Festa dell'Immacolata Concezione 8 December

Natale 25 December

Festa di Santo Stefano 26 December

Safe Travel

○ Pickpockets commonly work tourist sites and crowded train platforms, especially the stations of Cinque Terre.

○ Some Genoa *caruggi* (narrow streets) can feel somewhat unnerving, especially after dark. Take care in the zone west of Via San Luca and south to Piazza Banchi, where most street prostitution and accompanying vice concentrates.

○ Be mindful of strong currents when entering the sea. Watch out for *meduse* (jellyfish).

Dos & Don'ts

Greetings Greet people in shops, restaurants and bars with a *'buongiorno'* (good morning) or *'buonasera'* (good evening); kiss both cheeks and say *'come stai'* (how are you) to friends.

Asking for help Say *'mi scusi'* (excuse me) to attract attention; use *'permesso'* (permission) to pass someone in a crowded space.

Dress Cover shoulders, torso and thighs when visiting churches and dress smartly when eating out.

At the table Eat pasta with a fork, not a spoon; it's OK to eat pizza with your hands.

Toilets

○ Museums, department stores and train stations have public toilets. Otherwise, nip into a cafe or bar. It's polite to order something at the bar.

○ Some public toilets charge (€0.50 to €1).

Tourist Information

You'll find tourist offices in all the major towns along the coast.

○ Genoa has a tourist office in the airport and in the historic **centre** (☎010 557 29 03; www.visitgenoa.it; Via Garibaldi 12r; ⊗9am-6.20pm).

○ Online information about Cinque Terre is available at www.cinqueterre.it and www.cinqueterre.com. Every train station in Cinque Terre has an information office.

Visas

○ EU citizens do not need a visa to enter Italy.

○ Nationals of Australia, Canada, Israel, Japan, New Zealand, Switzerland and the USA do not need a visa for stays of up to 90 days.

○ Nationals of some other countries will need a Schengen tourist visa (see www.schengenvisainfo.com/tourist-schengen-visa).

○ Ensure your passport is valid for at least six months beyond your departure date from Italy.

Language

Regional dialects are an important part of identity in many parts of Italy, but you'll have no trouble being understood anywhere in the country if you stick to standard Italian, which is what we've used in this chapter.

The sounds used in Italian can all be found in English. If you read our pronunciation guides as if they were English, you'll be understood. The stressed syllables are indicated with italics. Note that *ai* is pronounced as in 'aisle', *ay* as in 'say', *ow* as in 'how', *dz* as the 'ds' in 'lids', and that *r* is a strong and rolled sound.

To enhance your trip with a phrasebook, visit lonelyplanet.com. Lonely Planet iPhone phrasebooks are available through the Apple App store.

Basics

Hello.
Buongiorno.   bwon·*jor*·no

Goodbye.
Arrivederci.   a·ree·ve·*der*·chee

How are you?
Come sta?   *ko*·me sta

Fine. And you?
Bene. E Lei?   *be*·ne e lay

Please.
Per favore.   per fa·*vo*·re

Thank you.
Grazie.   *gra*·tsye

Excuse me.
Mi scusi.   mee *skoo*·zee

Sorry.
Mi dispiace.   mee dees·*pya*·che

Yes./No.
Sì./No.   see/no

I don't understand.
Non capisco.   non ka·*pee*·sko

Do you speak English?
Parla inglese?   *par*·la een·*gle*·ze

Eating & Drinking

I'd like ...   *Vorrei ...*   vo·*ray* ...

a coffee   *un caffè*   oon ka·*fe*

a table   *un tavolo*   oon *ta*·vo·lo

the menu   *il menù*   eel me·*noo*

two beers   *due birre*   *doo*·e *bee*·re

What would you recommend?
Cosa mi consiglia?   *ko*·za mee kon·*see*·lya

That was delicious!
Era squisito!   *e*·ra skwee·*zee*·to

Cheers!
Salute!   sa·*loo*·te

Can you bring me the bill, please?
Mi porta il conto, per favore?   mee *por*·ta eel *kon*·to per fa·*vo*·re

Shopping

I'd like to buy ...
Vorrei comprare ...   vo·*ray* kom·*pra*·re ...

I'm just looking.
Sto solo guardando.   sto *so*·lo gwar·*dan*·do

How much is this?

Quanto costa	kwan·to kos·ta
questo?	kwe·sto

It's too expensive.

È troppo caro/	e tro·po ka·ro/
cara. (m/f)	ka·ra

Emergencies

Help!

Aiuto!	a·yoo·to

Call the police!

Chiami la	kya·mee la
polizia!	po·lee·tsee·a

Call a doctor!

Chiami un	kya·mee oon
medico!	me·dee·ko

I'm sick.

Mi sento male.	mee sen·to ma·le

I'm lost.

Mi sono perso/	mee so·no
persa. (m/f)	per·so/per·sa

Where are the toilets?

Dove sono i	do·ve so·no ee
gabinetti?	ga·bee·ne·tee

Time & Numbers

What time is it?

Che ora è?	ke o·ra e

It's (two) o'clock.

Sono le (due).	so·no le (doo·e)

morning	*mattina*	ma·tee·na
afternoon	*pomeriggio*	po·me·ree·jo
evening	*sera*	se·ra
yesterday	*ieri*	ye·ree
today	*oggi*	o·jee
tomorrow	*domani*	do·ma·nee

1	*uno*	oo·no
2	*due*	doo·e
3	*tre*	tre
4	*quattro*	kwa·tro
5	*cinque*	cheen·kwe
6	*sei*	say
7	*sette*	se·te
8	*otto*	o·to
9	*nove*	no·ve
10	*dieci*	dye·chee
100	*cento*	chen·to
1000	*mille*	mee·le

Transport & Directions

Where's ...?

Dove ...?	do·ve ...

What's the address?

Qual'è	kwa·le
l'indirizzo?	leen·dee·ree·tso

Can you show me (on the map)?

Può mostrarmi	pwo mos·trar·mee
(sulla pianta)?	(soo·la pyan·ta)

At what time does the ... leave?

A che ora	a ke o·ra
parte ...?	par·te ...

Does it stop at ...?

Si ferma a ...?	see fer·ma a ...

How do I get there?

Come ci si	ko·me chee see
arriva?	a·ree·va

bus	*autobus*	ow·to·boos
ticket	*biglietto*	bee·lye·to
timetable	*orario*	o·ra·ryo
train	*il treno*	eel tre·no

Behind the Scenes

Send Us Your Feedback

We love to hear from travellers – your comments help make our books better. We read every word, and we guarantee that your feedback goes straight to the authors. Visit **lonelyplanet.com/contact** to submit your updates and suggestions.

Note: We may edit, reproduce and incorporate your comments in Lonely Planet products such as guidebooks, websites and digital products, so let us know if you don't want your comments reproduced or your name acknowledged. For a copy of our privacy policy visit lonelyplanet.com/privacy.

Regis' Thanks

I'm grateful to countless Italians and expats who provided tips and insight into Liguria while on the road. Special thanks to Catherine Unger, Eugenio Bordoni and Arbaspàa staff in Cinque Terre. Hugs to Cassandra and our daughters Magdalena and Genevieve, who joined me for the great Ligurian adventure.

Acknowledgements

Cover photograph: Manarola, Anna Om/Shutterstock ©

This Book

This 1st edition of Lonely Planet's *Pocket Genoa & Cinque Terre* guidebook was researched and written by Regis St Louis. This guidebook was produced by the following:

Destination Editor
Anna Tyler

Senior Product Editor
Elizabeth Jones

Product Editor
Alison Ridgway

Regional Senior Cartographer Anthony Phelan

Book Designer
Fergal Condon

Assisting Editors Andrea Dobbin, Amy Lynch, Kate Morgan, Gabrielle Stefanos

Cover Researcher
Naomi Parker

Thanks to Imogen Bannister. Piotr Czajkowski, Kate Kiely, Benjamin Little, Diana Von Holdt

Index

See also separate subindexes for:

⊗ **Eating p157**

⊙ **Drinking p158**

☆ **Entertainment p158**

🔒 **Shopping p159**

Sights 000
Map Pages **000**

⊕ Shopping

Our Writer

Regis St Louis

Regis grew up in a small town in the American Midwest – the kind of place that fuels big dreams of travel – and he developed an early fascination with foreign dialects and world cultures. He spent his formative years learning Russian and a handful of Romance languages, which served him well on journeys across much of the globe. Regis has contributed to more than 50 Lonely Planet titles, covering destinations across six continents. His travels have taken him from the mountains of Kamchatka to remote island villages in Melanesia, and to many grand urban landscapes. When not on the road, he lives in New Orleans. Follow him on www.instagram.com/regisstlouis.

Published by Lonely Planet Global Limited
CRN 554153
1st edition – Feb 2020
ISBN 978 1 78868 335 7
© Lonely Planet 2020   Photographs © as indicated 2020
10 9 8 7 6 5 4 3 2 1
Printed in Singapore

The adventure continues on
lonelyplanet.com

Explore
Thorn Tree, the biggest and best online travel community

Share
with Lonely Planet on **Instagram, Facebook, Twitter, YouTube** and more

Shop
for guidebooks, eBooks, gift books and more

Book
flights, hotels, tours and travel insurance

Download our free app – Guides by Lonely Planet
City guides with offline maps, essential tips and top experiences curated by our experts.
APP STORE® & GOOGLE PLAY™

Stay in touch lonelyplanet.com/contact

AUSTRALIA The Malt Store, Level 3, 551 Swanston St, Carlton, Victoria 3053 ☎ 03 8379 8000

IRELAND Digital Depot, Roe Lane (off Thomas St), Digital Hub, Dublin 8, D08 TCV4

USA 155 Filbert Street, Suite 208, Oakland, CA 94607 ☎ 510 250 6400, toll free 800 275 8555

UK 240 Blackfriars Road, London SE1 8NW ☎ 020 3771 5100

 twitter.com/ lonelyplanet

 facebook.com/ lonelyplanet

 instagram.com/ lonelyplanet

 youtube.com/ lonelyplanet

Lonely planet

GET STRAIGHT TO THE HEART OF GENOA & CINQUE TERRE

Perfect for a short break or weekend away, this concise, practical and easy-to-use guide is packed with Genoa & Cinque Terre's best sights, itineraries and local secrets to help you create a memorable trip.

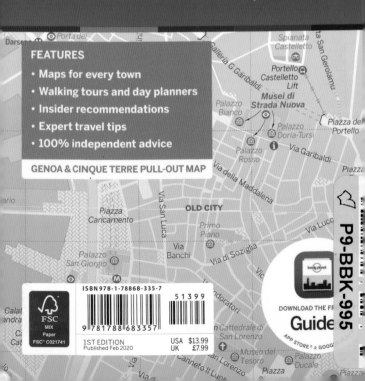

FEATURES

- Maps for every town
- Walking tours and day planners
- Insider recommendations
- Expert travel tips
- 100% independent advice

GENOA & CINQUE TERRE PULL-OUT MAP

ISBN 978-1-78868-335-7

51399

9 781788 683357

FSC
MIX
Paper
FSC® C021741

1ST EDITION
Published Feb 2020

USA $13.99
UK £7.99

DOWNLOAD THE FR
Guide
APP STORE® & GOOG

P9-BBK-995